BOW WOW WOW!

BOW WOW WOW!

Fetching Costumes for Your Fabulous Dog

Cathie Filian

LARK BOOKS

A Division of Sterling Publishing Co., Inc.
New York / London

DEVELOPMENT EDITOR
Deborah Morgenthal

PRODUCTION EDITOR
Linda Kopp

ART DIRECTOR
Kristi Pfeffer

ASSOCIATE ART DIRECTOR
Shannon Yokeley

ILLUSTRATOR
Orrin Lundgren

PROJECT PHOTOGRAPHER
Keith Wright

HOW-TO PHOTOGRAPHER
Zach Driscoll

COVER DESIGNER
Cindy LaBreacht

EDITORIAL ASSISTANT
Amanda Carestio

Library of Congress Cataloging-in-Publication Data

Filian, Cathie, 1970-
  Bow wow WOW! : fetching costumes for your fabulous dog / Cathie Filian. --
1st ed.
     p. cm.
  Includes index.
  ISBN-13: 978-1-60059-235-5 (PB-trade pbk. : alk. paper)
  ISBN-10: 1-60059-235-X (PB-trade pbk. : alk. paper)
  1. Costume. 2. Dogs--Equipment and supplies. I. Title.
  TT633.F55 2008
  646.4'78--dc22

                            2007050640

10 9 8 7 6 5 4 3 2 1

First Edition

Published by Lark Books, A Division of
Sterling Publishing Co., Inc.
387 Park Avenue South, New York, NY 10016

Text © 2008, Cathie Filian
Photography © 2008, Lark Books, unless otherwise specified
Illustrations © 2008, Lark Books, unless otherwise specified

Distributed in Canada by Sterling Publishing,
c/o Canadian Manda Group, 165 Dufferin Street
Toronto, Ontario, Canada M6K 3H6

Distributed in the United Kingdom by GMC Distribution Services,
Castle Place, 166 High Street, Lewes, East Sussex, England BN7 1XU

Distributed in Australia by Capricorn Link (Australia) Pty Ltd.,
P.O. Box 704, Windsor, NSW 2756 Australia

If you have questions or comments about this book, please contact:
Lark Books
67 Broadway
Asheville, NC 28801
828-253-0467

Manufactured in China

ISBN 13: 978-1-60059-235-5
ISBN 10: 1-60059-235-X

For information about custom editions, special sales, premium and corporate purchases, please
contact Sterling Special Sales Department at 800-805-5489 or specialsales@sterlingpub.com.

Contents

No dogs were made to feel foolish during the creation of this book.

Introduction

I had so much fun writing this book. As I was making all the dog costumes—sewing, gluing, and attaching tiny rhinestones into the wee hours of the night—I kept thinking about how my fashion design professors would either be horrified or explode with applause at my interpretation of a Sea Creature (page 90). I thought about my 99-year-old grandmother. What would she think of my Saucy Red Hat Ladies (page 56)? And my Catholic high school home economics teacher—would she be appalled by my naughty Biker Babe costume (page 31) or marvel at my stitching?

My experience from "test walks" is that these costumes garner a wonderful mix of double takes and glowing praise from passersby. With a few simple patterns, some basic sewing skills, and a little craftiness, you too can create amazing dog outfits that will turn heads. First, I'll tell you how to create the basic patterns: the doggie dress for the gals and a cape pattern for the boys. With only a few adaptations, these patterns serve as the basis for every costume in this book. And then to add those oh-so-important finishing touches, I'll show you how to use found objects and store-bought accessories—such as doll-sized hats and children's toys—to take your dog costumes over the top.

Don't sew or don't have the time? Not a problem. I've included a number of no-sew costumes so no dog goes unrobed. For example, check out Jail Bird (page 110) and Skully (page 88). Sprinkled throughout this book you'll also find plenty of quick and easy doggy accessory ideas for creating or customizing those everyday necessities—leashes, collars, and bandanas.

Unless they were fools to begin with.

Designing these costumes brought back pleasant memories of dogs from my past and present. When I was a little girl, my sister and I would dress Little Bit (our Yorkie) in doll clothing and pretend she was a princess. And I smile when I think of our loveable Old English Sheepdog, Grover, and how funny he would look in one of my new creations. Then there was Maggie, our spunky Dalmatian and the true inspiration for the Fire Patrol costume (page 44).

As I tried endless costumes on my dear little Max, I recalled all the family jokes and stories about how Max's closet was as big as mine, which is almost true—he does have more than 20 hats, a down jacket…and a princess costume. And then I realized that what really mattered was that Max and I were having fun together and that he loved playing dress up just as much as I did.

I hope the projects inspire you to create your own pet costumes. Let the basic patterns be springboards for your own imagination and creativity, and have fun getting crafty with your pooch.

Cathie Filian

Basics

Getting Started

Does your pup long to be a deep-sea pirate or a flirty French maid? How about a classic vampire or a Beverly Hills socialite? Deciding which costume to make is the hardest part of making your own dog costumes, but try using your pooch's personality for hints.

Your dog costume can be as simple or complex as you'd like. Perhaps your four-legged-friend yearns to show his team spirit; a quick, no-sew T-shirt costume is an easy option for you and your pooch. For something more involved, try creating one of the fabulous costumes in this book or alter the basic patterns to make one of your own designs. Once you've picked a costume, all you need to get started are your imagination, fabric, and a few basic sewing supplies.

RESEARCHING COSTUMES

My first step in designing a costume is research. I explore the history of the costume by perusing encyclopedias along with historical and vintage books. I watch movies for inspiration, and browse magazines and the paint section at hardware stores for color palettes and textures. Lastly, I swatch fabrics and trims. After gathering all my research materials, I create a collage using the clippings and swatches—and then I go shopping.

CHOOSING FABRIC

I am a fabric addict. I have an entire room filled with fabric and ribbons. You can use just about any fabric for these costumes. Go wild with the outer fabrics, and stick to non-stretchy, soft cotton fabrics for the linings. When I set out to collect fabrics, my first stop is my fabric stash, and my second is the fabric shop. For the costumes in this book, I used some fabrics and trims I've had for years while others were newly purchased just for the occasion. So don't worry if you can't find the exact fabric I used. Think of my fabric choices as inspiration, and look for similar ones. If you feel like you have exhausted your fabric store options, turn to the internet. I love shopping online and have purchased some amazing fabrics, buttons, and trims.

SEWING SUPPLIES

To create the costumes in this book, you'll need a few simple sewing tools and supplies. Before beginning a project, take the time to gather these necessary items for your sewing kit.

Basic Sewing Tool Kit

- Tape measure
- Needle and thread
- Elastic
- Hook-and-loop tape
- Safety and straight pins
- Glue gun and glue sticks
- Sewing machine
- Iron and ironing board

COSTUME CLEANING

Just like children, some dogs will be harder on their clothes than others. There are a variety of ways to deal with a costume that needs cleaning. Costumes that are not washable can be lint rolled, spot cleaned, sprayed with a fabric freshener, and air dried. Costumes that are washable should be washed by hand or on your washer's gentle cycle, then line dried. If you need a costume that can be cleaned, be sure to use washable fabrics and trims. Trims should be attached with fabric glue or sewn. You can also add pinbacks to small accessories and props so these items can be removed before washing.

No-Sew Costumes

Need to make a big statement but don't have a lot of time? T-shirt costumes are the perfect pick for dogs, and dog owners, on the go. Purchase a plain T-shirt from pet stores or from online T-shirt suppliers for just a few dollars, then transform your T-shirt using fabric paints and glue (and maybe a teeny bit of stitching) to create anything from a queen bee to a spooky skeleton. Look for the No Sew icon throughout the book for more great design ideas.

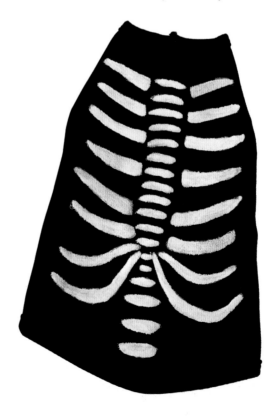

SIZING UP YOUR PUP

Dogs are like snowflakes: no two are alike—or the same size. I have developed two patterns, the doggie dress and the cape pattern, that serve as the basis for all the costumes in this book. The pattern sizes I use are based on retail dog apparel but are extremely easy to customize. A few simple measurements taken ahead of time will ensure you get the best fit.

To properly measure your dog, place the end of a tape measure at the base of the dog's neck and stretch it across the back to the base of the tail. Once you have this measurement, find where your dog fits on the chart or simply look for your dog's breed to find the correct size.

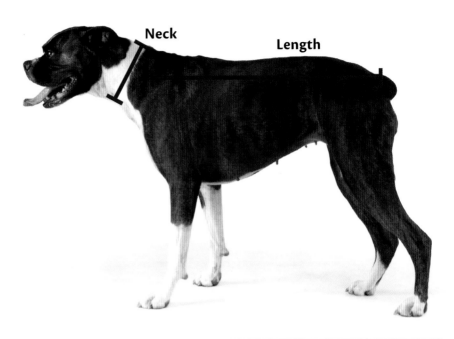

Neck   **Length**

GENERAL SIZE GUIDE

Size	Breed		Length	Weight
Extra Small	Smaller Chihuahua Toy Poodles	Teacup Breeds Small puppies	6 to 9 inches (15.2 to 22.9 cm)	2 to 6 pounds (.9 to 2.7 kg)
Small	Chihuahua Dachshund Maltese Miniature Pinscher	Pomeranian Shih Tzu Yorkshire Terrier	10 to 13 inches (25.4 to 33 cm)	7 to 12 pounds (3.2 to 5.4 kg)
Medium	Beagle Bichon Frise Boston Terrier Cavalier King Charles Cocker Spaniel Jack Russell Terrier	Miniature Poodle Pekingese Pug Scottish Terrier West Highland Terrier	14 to 18 inches (35.6 to 45.7 cm)	13 to 20 pounds (5.9 to 9.1 kg)
Wide Medium	English Bulldog Corgi Miniature Schnauzer		14 to 21 inches (35.6 to 53.3 cm)	13 to 30 pounds (5.9 to 13.6 kg)
Large	American Bulldog Australian Shepherd Collie English Setter Greyhound	Pointer Springer Spaniel Staffordshire Bull Terrier Whippet	22 to 26 inches (55.9 to 66 cm)	40 to 70 pounds (18.2 to 31.8 kg)
Extra Large	Airedale Terrier Boxer Dalmatian Doberman Pinscher German Shepherd Golden Retriever	Husky Irish Setter Labrador Retriever Standard Poodle Weimaraner	22 to 31 inches (55.9 to 78.7 cm)	50 to 80 pounds (22.7 to 36.3 kg)

The Patterns

The doggy dress and cape patterns are the basis for every costume in this book. Once you've mastered these basic patterns, you'll be off and running. Hats, shoe, and ruffle patterns will help your hound complete his look, because, even for dogs, every outfit needs accessories.

Using the patterns is easy. First, you'll need to use a copy machine to enlarge the patterns based on the size of your dog. For larger-sized dogs, you might need to enlarge the pattern in sections and then tape the pieces together. Because all sizes are approximate, it's a good idea to place the paper pattern piece on your dog or create a pattern from muslin fabric before you cut into your costume fabric. To find out approximately how much fabric you'll need, refer to the yardage charts.

DOGGIE DRESS

Creating the doggie dress is as easy as learning sit, stay, and shake. The pattern can be customized to any size dog, although it works especially well for smaller-sized breeds. With the addition of trim, buttons, embellishments, and fun fabrics, this pattern can be stitched into many different costumes. You can make anything from a cowgirl or a French maid to a glamorous valley girl and a spunky witch. The sky is the limit so get creative and get stitching.

Stuff You Need

Dress pattern (page 116)
Copy machine
Fabric
Single-fold bias tape
Optional embellishments:
    patches, trim, buttons, bows,
    rhinestones, silk flowers
Basic Sewing Tool Kit (page 9)

Instructions

1. Start by first cutting out the paper pattern pieces. Fold the fabric, right sides together, and pin the top front pattern piece to the fabric, aligning the pattern fold line to the fold in the fabric. Pin the top back pattern piece to the fabric in the same direction as the front piece (photo A) and then cut out all the pieces. Repeat this process for the lining and the skirt pattern pieces, making the skirt longer or shorter to suit your pooch.

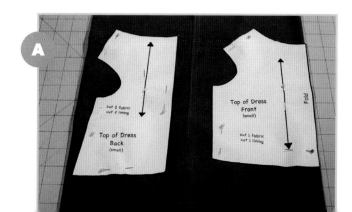

2. Working right sides together, sew the top front and top back pieces together at the shoulder (photo B) and side seams (photo C) using a ⅝-inch (1.6 cm) seam allowance. Repeat for the lining. Press the seams open so they lay flat.

3. Fold the skirt piece in half lengthwise, right sides together.

4. Sew up the side seams of the skirt piece, and trim the seams. Turn the skirt piece right side out and press.

5. Sew a long gathering stitch across the top of the skirt piece. Pull the threads to gather the top of the skirt (photo D).

6. Pin the skirt piece along the bottom edge of the right side of the top front piece (photo E). Stay stitch the skirt in place.

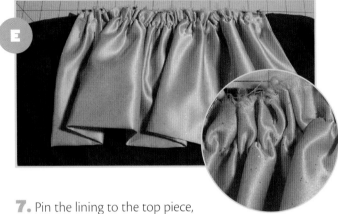

7. Pin the lining to the top piece, right sides together, catching the skirt edge in the seam. Sew around the outer edge of the top piece, leaving a 5-inch (12.7 cm) opening on the side for turning.

8. Trim the corners (photo F), clip around the curves (photo G), and turn right side out.

9. Press, hand stitch the 5-inch (12.7 cm) opening closed, and topstitch around the outer edge if desired.

10. Working on the right side of the dress, pin and sew the single-fold bias tape around the armhole openings (photo H). Trim and clip the seams to create a smooth curve.

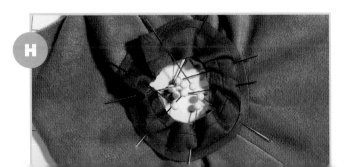

11. Fold the bias tape to the lining side, press, and pin. Hand stitch the bias tape to the lining (photo I).

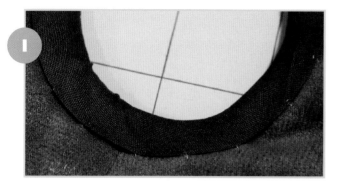

12. Sew the hook-and-loop tape to the opening on the dress. Stitch the rough side on one side of the dress opening and the soft side on the other side so that they overlap to close (photo J). Now for the fun part: embellishments!

DRESS PATTERN YARDAGE CHART			
Size	Dress Top	Skirt	Lining
Extra Small	½ yard (.5 m)	¼ yard (.2 m)	½ yard (.5 m)
Small	⅓ yard (.3 m)	⅓ yard (.3 m)	⅓ yard (.3 m)
Medium	⅜ yard (.3 m)	½ yard (.5 m)	⅜ yard (.3 m)
Wide Medium	½ yard (.5 m)	⅝ yard (.6 m)	½ yard (.5 m)
Large	½ yard (.5 m)	⅝ yard (.6 m)	½ yard (.5 m)
Extra Large	⅝ yard (.6 m)	¾ yard (.7 m)	⅝ yard (.6 m)

CANINE CAPE

Well suited for canines both great and small, the cape pattern can be transformed into many different costumes by simply layering fabrics and trims. You can make a traditional cape costume, like a vampire or a devil or go wild with a sea creature or a biker babe. With side flaps that fasten around the dog's belly and keep the costume in place, this pattern works especially well for larger dogs and is great for making warm gear for cold weather.

Stuff You Need

Cape pattern (page 119)
Copy machine
Fabric
Optional embellishments:
    patches, trim, buttons, bows,
    and rhinestones
Basic Sewing Tool Kit (page 9)

Instructions

1. Once you've cut out the pattern, pin the cape pattern piece to the fabric, aligning the fold line on the pattern to the fold in the fabric. Repeat for the lining. Pin the collar pattern piece to the fabric, and cut out the pattern pieces.

2. If you'd like to customize the cape, add decorative layers of fabric by duplicating sections of the pattern. Turn under any raw edges that might be exposed, and pin the design pieces to the right side of the cape. Topstitch the design pieces in place (photo A).

3. Pin two of the side flap pieces together, with right sides facing. Sew around the two long edges and one short edge. Clip the corners, (photo B) turn the flap right side out, and press. Repeat this process with the two remaining flap pieces.

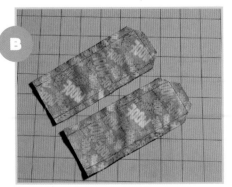

4. Pin the collar pieces right sides together, and sew around the entire collar, leaving an opening for turning. Clip the seams, (photo C) turn the collar right side out, and press.

5. Working on the right side of the cape, pin the collar to the center top and the side flaps to each side just below the curve so that the collar and the side flaps lay on top of the cape (photo D).

6. Working right sides together, pin the lining to the cape (photo E). Sew around the entire cape, catching the side flaps and the collar in the seam and leaving an opening for turning. Clip the seam and corners.

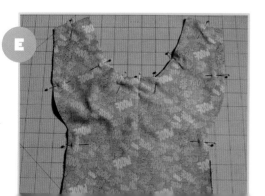

7. Turn the cape right side out, press, and sew the opening closed.

8. Sew the hook-and-loop tape to the side flaps. Stitch the rough side on one side of the flap and the soft side on the other flap so the pieces overlap to close (photo F).

9. Using the same technique, sew hook-and-loop tape to the chest flaps. Embellish your cape for a fun, customized look that will suit your dog's unique personality.

CAPE PATTERN YARDAGE CHART

Size	Cape Fabric	Lining
Extra Small	½ yard (.5 m)	½ yard (.5 m)
Small	½ yard (.5 m)	½ yard (.5 m)
Medium	¾ yard (.7 m)	¾ yard (.7 m)
Wide Medium/Large	⅞ yard (.8 m)	⅞ yard (.8 m)
Extra Large	1 yard (.9 m)	1 yard (.9 m)

Adding Accessories

It's all in the details, and dog costumes are no exception. Adding accessories and props really makes these outfits come alive. To deck out your pet from head to paw, I've included patterns for head gear, neckwear, shoes, and ruffles. Dollar stores and thrift stores can be gold mines for finding inexpensive props and accessories. The doll-making section at your local craft or fabric store usually has lots of hats, funny eyes, and small props that can be used to really trick out a costume. I look for lightweight items that can be attached easily with hot glue, fabric glues, or by sewing.

HATS

Hats are one accessory that can really make a fashion statement. You can easily create your own from scratch or alter doll- and child-sized items to create a one-of-a-kind chapeau. As with the other patterns, you'll need to first enlarge or reduce the pattern pieces to fit your dog. For a snug fit, you'll also need elastic to create a chin strap that will secure the hat on Fido's head. Refer to the guide to see how much elastic to use based on the size of your furry friend.

ELASTIC CHIN STRAP SIZE GUIDE

Extra Small	7 inches (17.8 cm)
Small	7 inches (17.8 cm)
Medium	8 inches (20.3 cm)
Fuller Medium	9 inches (22.9 cm)
Large	10 inches (25.4 cm)
Extra Large	12 inches (30.5 cm)

Peak Hat

The peak hat is perfect for creating a pirate or maid hat. If you add a little tulle, this pattern can even be transformed into a doggie bridal veil.

Stuff You Need

Peak hat pattern (page 121)
Fabric scrap
¼ yard (.2 m) of ribbon,
    1 inch (2.5 cm) wide
Elastic
Basic Sewing Tool Kit (page 9)

Instructions

1. After you cut out the pattern pieces, pin them to the fabric. For printed fabric, you may need to adjust the fold line so your print is going in the proper direction. Cut two pieces.

2. Place the two pieces right sides together, and sew around all the edges, leaving an opening for turning. Turn the fabric right side out, and hand stitch the opening closed.

3. Add support by sewing a strip of ribbon down the center (photo A).

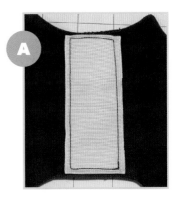

4. Cut a piece of elastic using the Elastic Chin Strap Size Guide. Sew one end of the elastic to the side edge of the center of the hat and the other end to the opposite side (photo B).

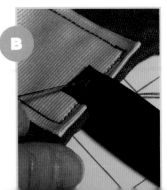

5. Bring the front and back of the hat together at the top, and hand stitch along the top seam. If your hat needs even more personality, add festive embellishments like trim, pom-poms, or flowers (photo C).

Store-Bought Hats

Creating a dog hat from a doll- or child-sized hat is as easy as adding ribbon or elastic straps and embellishing. Follow these simple guidelines:

For straw hats, poke two holes on each side, thread elastic through, and knot the ends. Secure the elastic with a drop of hot glue, if needed.

For fabric hats, sew elastic or ribbon to the sides.

For plastic hats, drill two holes on each side using either a drill or an awl. Add elastic or ribbon, and you've got yourself a dog hat.

Decorate your hat with paint, feathers, ribbon, toys, small patches, buttons, bows, and rhinestones.

Cone Hat

The cone hat is perfect for a witch's hat or, with a few adjustments, a fun and funky clown hat. This style is also a treat to embellish; mix and match trims and fabrics to really customize the look.

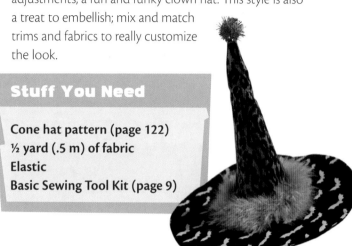

Stuff You Need

Cone hat pattern (page 122)
½ yard (.5 m) of fabric
Elastic
Basic Sewing Tool Kit (page 9)

Instructions

1. Pin the pattern to the fabric. For printed fabric, you may need to adjust the fold line so your print is going in the proper direction. Cut out the pieces.

2. Place the two pieces right sides together, and sew down the two side seams. Turn the fabric right side out and press, if needed. Fold the piece in half lengthwise, and sew up the side seam.

3. Make a pattern for the brim on a piece of paper. Draw a circle that measures 10 inches (25.4 cm) in diameter, or just trace around a large plate. Draw a circle in the center that measures 2¾ inches (7 cm) in diameter. These measurements will work for most dogs, but you should measure Fido's head just to be sure.

4. Using your brim pattern, cut two 10-inch (25.4 cm) circles of fabric, and remove the small center circle from each piece.

5. Place the circles right sides together, and sew around the outside edge. Turn the fabric right side out and press, if needed.

6. Working with right sides together, sew the brim to the cone. Zigzag stitch the edge to prevent fraying, if needed. Clip the seam around the curve (photo A).

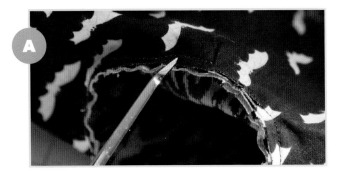

7. Create a chin strap with elastic based on the guide. Sew one end of the elastic to each side edge of the hat. Sew or use fabric glue to attach embellishments as desired.

Tip: Omit the brim to create a clown-style hat perfect for your little entertainer.

Base Hat

The base hat is a foundation for embellishing. You can add just about anything to the base: flowers for a headband, horns for a devil, or even pipe cleaners for antennas.

Stuff You Need

Base hat pattern (page 121)
Fabric scrap
Elastic
Basic Sewing Tool Kit (page 9)

Instructions

1. Pin the pattern to the fabric, and cut out two pieces.

2. Place the two pieces right sides together, and sew around the edges, leaving an opening for turning. Turn the fabric right side out. Hand stitch the opening closed.

3. Following the guide, cut a piece of elastic for the chin strap. Sew one end of the elastic to each side edge of the hat (photo A). Customize your hat until you get just the right look. Add trim, horns, twisted pipe cleaners, pins, ribbon, or other embellishments.

RUFFLES

Ruffles are the perfect way to add a little fluff and style to your pup's attire. Use coordinating ruffles as the finishing touch to a fabulous dog costume or stack multiple ruffles for a look that can stand alone; either way, your dog will be ready for her close-up.

Stuff You Need

Fabric
Elastic
Basic Sewing Tool Kit (page 9)

1. Wrap a piece of elastic around the lower portion of your dog's leg to get the correct elastic measurement, pulling the elastic so it is secure, but not tight. Cut one piece of elastic to this measurement.

2. To create a skinny ruffle, cut a strip of fabric that is 3 inches (7.6 cm) wide and three times the length of the elastic. To make a wide ruffle, cut a strip of fabric that is 6 inches (15.2 cm) wide and three times the length of the elastic. Working right sides together, sew the fabric along the long side seams to make a tube shape, and turn right side out (photo A).

3. Thread the elastic through the tube, securing the elastic at each end of the tube with a pin. Sew the ends together, catching the elastic in the seam (photo B). Trim the ends and repeat the process for as many ruffles as you want.

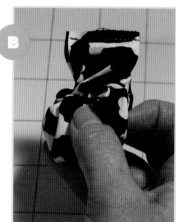

I feel pretty, oh so pretty...

BANDANAS

Bandanas are the ultimate doggie accessory, and they are a snap to make. You only need a small amount of fabric and just a few minutes to create one or maybe even two. They are ideal for using up small scraps of fabric and trims, or you can purchase specialty fabrics for just the right canine occasion.

So many fantastic fabrics, so little time. Dog-themed fabrics run the gamut from cutesy and silly to masculine and modern. Bandanas are a great way for Fido to express his holiday spirit. Other fabrics are better suited for everyday style. You can choose prints that reflect your personality or make one with a traditional bandana print.

This pattern offers two options for maximum bandana flexibility. You can create a bandana that slides onto your dog's collar so you won't have to worry about it coming untied. The second option allows for a quick change with a handy hook-and-loop tape closure—perfect for the doggie fashion diva. As with the other patterns, you'll have to enlarge or reduce the pattern on a copier for smaller and larger sizes, although there's really no wrong size for a bandana.

Stuff You Need

For the collar bandana:
Bandana pattern #1 (page 123)
12 x 24-inch (30.5 x 61 cm) piece of fabric

For the hook-and-loop bandana:
Bandana pattern #2 (page 123)
Small piece of fabric
Sew-on hook-and-loop squares

Optional Embellishments: trims, buttons,
   rhinestones, patches, or bows
Basic Sewing Tool Kit (page 9)

Instructions

1. Once you've cut out your pattern, pin the pieces to the fabric. Align the pattern in the proper direction for the print on your fabric, and cut two pieces.

2. Place the two cut pieces right sides together and pin around the outer edge, leaving a 3-inch (7.6 cm) opening at the top for turning. Sew around the edge using a ⅝-inch (1.6 cm) seam allowance.

3. Turn the bandana right side out and press, if needed. Hand stitch the opening closed. If you're making the hook-and-loop bandana, skip to step 5.

4. For the collar bandana, fold the top edge down 1½ inches (3.8 cm) and press. Stitch along the edge of the flap, creating a pocket for the collar to slip through (photo A). Embellish to your liking and slide the collar through the pocket opening.

5. For the hook-and-loop bandana, topstitch around the outer edge (photo B).

6. Sew hook-and-loop squares to the ends of the bandana so the ends will flap over and connect (photo C). For the fashion-forward pooch, consider embellishing the bandana.

Tip: Create a holiday-themed bandana by embroidering details on a solid-colored bandana, like this skull embroidery designed by Gina Zycher.

SHOES

Dog shoes make quite the fashion statement, and they're so easy to make. Since you use felt as the base, they are also soft and comfy for your four-legged friend. You can even lengthen the basic shoe pattern to create some snazzy boots.

Stuff You Need

Shoe pattern (page 124)
Felt
Hook-and-loop tape
Additional decorative fabric scraps
Basic Sewing Tool Kit (page 9)

Instructions

1. Start by measuring the height and width of the thickest part of your dog's lower leg. Add 1 inch (2.5 cm) to the width, and create a pattern using the shoe template as a guide.

2. Cut the pattern pieces out of felt.

3. Add details like socks, buckles, or laces by sewing or gluing additional fabrics, buttons, and trims onto the top of the shoe piece (photo A).

4. Sew the hook-and-loop tape down the sides of the shoe. Stitch the rough side on one side and the soft side on the other so they overlap to close.

COLLARS AND LEASHES

Most of us have basic fashion essentials that we wear each day—like a watch. But just because something is a functional necessity doesn't mean it has to be dull. For instance, collars and leashes (necessities for your dog) can be easily customized with just a few supplies. Mix and match ribbons, trims, and embellishments to complement your pup's outfit or create a collar that can stand alone, in all its fashionable glory.

Look for the Canine Couture columns throughout the book for design ideas that will let your pup strut her ultra-feminine stuff (page 51); rock on with spunky style (page 99); or relax after a hard day (page 37). Other design suggestions will help your pooch live it up Vegas style (page 25); display some everyday style (page 63); or get in the spooky holiday spirit (page 83).

Stuff You Need

Store-bought collar or leash (the ones made of webbing work best)
Embellishments: theme-printed ribbons, sequins, solid ribbons, pom-poms, upholstery edging, snap tape, marabou feather trim, bridal tulle, fringe, faux leather
Basic Sewing Tool Kit (page 9)

Instructions

1. Measure the length and width of the collar/leash (excluding the buckles, holes, clips, and handle), and choose a ribbon or trim that is appropriately sized. You can use different sizes of ribbons and trims and layer them on top of each other.

2. Attach the ribbon or trim by gluing, hand sewing, or using a sewing machine.

If you decide to use glue, try a heavy-duty fabric glue and then clamp the trim to the collar or leash with clothespins until it's thoroughly dry (photo A).

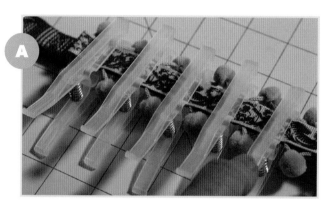

If you use a sewing machine, experiment with different feet and settings until you find one that suits your needs. I like using a zipper foot to get really close to the edge.

3. Sew or use glue to attach additional design elements like patches, flowers, bows, buttons, scrapbooking embellishments, sequins, rhinestones, and marabou trim, or all of the above.

Viva Las Vegas

A little much? Maybe.
Over the top? Probably.
Absolutely fabulous?
You betcha'!
A drive-through romance,
your pooch's inner card shark,
and (who else?) the King
form the basis for this wacky
group of costumes inspired
by Sin City.

Canine Couture

Is your pooch in the market for something a little extravagant? Nothing says Vegas like rhinestones and feather trim, and that's exactly what you get with the ruffled explosion that is Fluff. Indulge your canine's competitive nature with game-board pieces in Got Game Name or his soulful side with Lounge Hound.

Fluff

Puppy needs a new pair of shoes.

S₁ A₁ D₂ I₁ E₁

Got Game Name

Lounge Hound

Never drink in Vegas.

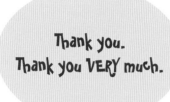

Thank you. Thank you VERY much.

Hound Dog

HOUND DOG

Materials

CAPE

Cape pattern (page 119)
White satin-backed shantung
1-inch (2.5 cm) gold fringe
Gold, red, and blue sequin trims
Red looped sequin trim
Iron-on studded patches and
    musical clefs
White cotton
Hound dog patch

WIG

Black faux fur
Elastic

ACCESSORIES

Sunglasses

SUPPLIES & TOOLS

Basic Sewing Tool Kit (page 9)
Dark fabric ink-jet transfers

SIZE PICTURED: EXTRA LARGE

Instructions

CAPE

1. Sew the cape following the cape pattern instructions (page 14). For the collar, I used the satin side of the fabric, and for the cape, I used the shantung side.

2. Hot glue or sew the gold fringe and gold trim around the outer edge of the cape. Add a strip of red looped sequin trim ½-inch (1.3 cm) in from the gold trim.

3. In the center of the cape, iron on the studded patches. In the lower corners, iron on the music patches (photo A).

4. Using ink-jet fabric transfers, create a personalized patch; mine says "Hound Dog," but yours could say anything you like. Iron the transfer on the bottom center of the cape, and glue gold sequin trim around the edge of the patch. Add strips of red, blue, and gold sequin trim across the cape just above the patch.

5. Hot glue or sew the red and gold trim around the edge of the collar.

POMPADOUR WIG

6. Cut two elongated triangles of faux black fur.

7. Lay the two pieces together with right sides facing, and stitch along the outside edge, leaving a small opening for turning.

8. Turn the fabric right side out, stuff the shape with batting or fabric scraps, and stitch the opening closed.

9. Curl back the tip of the wig and tack it with a few stitches. Following the elastic size guide (page 16), cut and then attach elastic to both sides of the wig.

10. Add some fancy "rock and roll" glasses, and your pooch is ready for the stage.

Hound Dog Tip

Use dark fabric ink-jet transfers even when working on light fabrics. They create a clear image, and they don't need to be reversed.

Wedding

The Bride

Materials

DRESS

Dress pattern (page 116)
Cream jacquard
Cream double-ruffle lace
Pearl lace trim
Paw print rhinestones

VEIL

Peak hat pattern (page 121)
Cream jacquard
Cream tulle
Double ruffle lace
Pearl trim
Sheer ribbon rosettes

ACCESSORIES

Flower bouquet

SUPPLIES & TOOLS

Basic Sewing Tool Kit (page 9)

SIZE PICTURED: MEDIUM

Instructions

DRESS

1. Sew the top and skirt portion of the dress as described in the doggie dress pattern (page 11).

2. Attach cream ruffled trim around the neck, waist, and hemline. For extra pizzazz, add pearl trim along the top of the ruffle.

3. Use an iron to heat-set the rhinestones in the shape of a paw print in the center of the dress and in the corner of the skirt (photo A).

4. Wrap the stems of a small bouquet of flowers with ribbon, and hand sew or hot glue it to the waist of the dress. Add two ribbon rosettes to the neck and waistline.

VEIL

5. Sew the veil as described in the peak hat pattern (page 16). Don't sew the top closed until after you have attached the tulle.

6. Create the veil by layering two 10 x 50-inch (25.4 x 127 cm) pieces of cream tulle on top of each other.

7. Gather the tulle across the long edge until it measures 4 inches (10.2 cm). Sew the gathered tulle to the back of the hat.

Bride Tip

Got an old prom dress in your closet? Re-craft it into a fancy dress for your pooch.

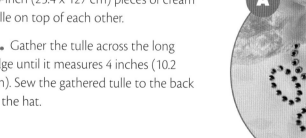

The Groom

Materials

CAPE
Cape pattern (page 119)
Black satin fabric
Cream jacquard fabric
Antique lilac satin fabric
(cummerbund)
Black sequin trim
Black and gold trim
Paw print ribbon
2 dog buttons
Silk flower

HAT
Doll-sized top hat
Black and gold trim

SUPPLIES & TOOLS
Basic Sewing Tool Kit (page 9)

SIZE PICTURED: MEDIUM

Instructions

CAPE

1. Following the cape pattern but omitting the collar, cut out the cape pattern from the black satin fabric.

2. On top of the fabric, layer a rectangle of the cream jacquard to create a tuxedo shirt.

3. Create a cummerbund by sewing a wide tube of lilac satin. Iron pleats into the tube, and sew the cummerbund across the center of the cape (photo A). Continue sewing the costume following the cape instructions (page 14).

4. Hot glue or sew black sequin trim across the top and along the sides of the tux shirt. Using paw print ribbon and scraps from the cummerbund, create a bow and sew the bow onto the cape at the center neck.

5. Attach two buttons just under the bow, and hot glue a small silk flower on the chest (photo at left).

HAT

6. Poke two holes in the sides of a doll-sized top hat. Cut a piece of elastic to the appropriate size, thread it through the holes, and tie off the ends with a knot, adding a drop of glue for extra security.

7. Hot glue black and gold trim around the base.

Groom Tip

Need a four-legged ring bearer? Sew a ribbon to the center of the costume and tie the rings to the ribbon. To avoid any doggy mishaps, consider using fake rings.

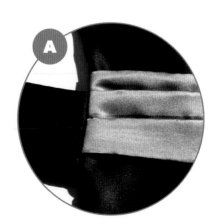

Only bikers know why dogs stick their heads out car windows.

Biker Babe

Materials

CAPE

Cape pattern (page 119)
Light tan fabric
Gray lace fabric
Black vinyl (pants)
Black fringe
Flaming skull cotton fabric
Iron-on tattoo patch
Dog bone license plate

BIKINI

Light tan fabric
Gray lace fabric
Pillow stuffing
Black vinyl
Black lace
Black fringe
Black vinyl grommet trim
Spider button

BOOTS

Shoe pattern (page 124)
Red felt
Black vinyl
Black vinyl grommet trim
Black fringe

SUPPLIES & TOOLS

Basic Sewing Tool Kit (page 9)

SIZE PICTURED: MEDIUM

Instructions

CAPE

1. Begin by cutting out the cape pattern from the tan fabric, omitting the collar. In the center of the tan fabric, attach the iron-on tattoo patch.

2. Cut the cape pattern from the gray lace. Place the lace on the "tattoo" side of the tan fabric.

3. Sewing through both fabric layers, stitch around the tattoo. Use detail scissors to cut out the lace, exposing the tattoo (photo A). Continue assembling the cape following the cape pattern instructions (page 14).

4. On the bottom half of the tan/lace fabric, layer and then attach the black vinyl to create the pants.

5. Sew the fringe around the outer and top edges of the pants.

6. Hot glue a bone-shaped license plate to the corner of the pants.

BIKINI

7. Cut a strip of black vinyl and hot glue it to the costume. Glue black lace and fringe trim across the top of the bikini, and add grommet trim along the bottom and sides. Sew a spider button in the center of the bikini (photo B).

A

B

Boots

8. Follow the instructions for the shoe pattern (page 22), adding black vinyl to create a boot tip.

9. Glue on some grommet trim, and sew black fringe across the top of the boot.

Biker Babe Tip

Got the tattoo blues? If you can't find a tattoo patch, just make your own! Use ink-jet fabric transfers, printable fabric, or paint your own radical design.

Poker Time

Materials

CAPE

Cape pattern (page 119)
Green felt
Card and dice cotton fabric
    (lining, collar, and flaps)
Playing cards
Black sequin trim
Red sequin trim
Poker chips

ACCESSORIES

Toy sunglasses
Green visor

SUPPLIES & TOOLS

Basic Sewing Tool Kit (page 9)

SIZE PICTURED: EXTRA LARGE

Instructions

CAPE

1. Sew the cape as described in the cape pattern, using the green felt for the top and the card fabric for the lining (page 14).

2. Using hot glue, attach two playing cards on the corners of each collar. Around each card, add sequin trim and a poker chip. Hot glue or hand stitch trim around the collar (photo A).

3. Hot glue a row of five cards and a few poker chips down the center of the cape.

4. Create four hands of cards by hot gluing a set of five cards at each corner of the cape. Add a small stack of poker chips next to each hand of cards (photo B).

5. Add steely blue sunglasses or a green visor to keep the other players guessing (optional).

Poker Time Tip ♦

Poker not your game? How about football? You can easily transform this costume into a football field by painting a field onto the felt with white fabric paint. Add small football patches and a couple of toy players.

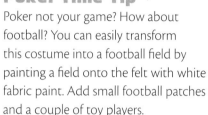

Doggy Do-Gooders

Got a goody two (or four!) shoes on your hands? Or maybe just a brownnoser? Either way, be sure to dress your canine crusader in the finest duds. Helping out at the hospital or saving lives, your pooch will look super cute no matter the mission.

Canine Couture

When he's not busy saving the planet, your little well-wisher needs rest and recreation. If America's favorite pastime is his game, deck him out with the patriotic Play Ball, or try First and Ten if football is more his fancy. With a cute Scotty button, Mad about Plaid is the perfect off-duty look for your little prepster, or give Holiday Glitz a go, with buttons, sequins, and double-ruffle trim to help him spread holiday cheer.

Play Ball

Mad about Plaid

First and Ten

Holiday Glitz

Candy Striper

There's got to be a better way to find an eligible doctor.

Materials

DRESS & APRON
Dress pattern (page 116)
Red and white pillow ticking
4-inch (10.2 cm) pleated
  eyelet trim
White gathered lace with red
  embroidered hearts
Nurse buttons

HAT
Peak hat pattern (page 121)
Red and white pillow ticking
White gathered lace with red
  embroidered hearts

ACCESSORIES
Basket filled with buttons,
  small toys, bones,
  newspaper, and heart trim

SUPPLIES & TOOLS
Basic Sewing Tool Kit
  (page 9)

SIZE PICTURED: MEDIUM

Instructions

DRESS
1. Cut out the pattern pieces from the red and white pillow ticking fabric.

2. Add a layer of the wide eyelet trim to the top of the skirt and a small section of trim to the top of the dress to create the apron. Sew the top and skirt portions of the dress following the doggy dress pattern (page 11).

3. Sew the ruffled heart trim on both sides of the top of the apron to create the faux apron ties. Sew the ruffled heart trim around the edge of the hem.

4. Hand stitch nurse's buttons to the front of the dress (photo A).

HAT
5. Sew the hat as described in the peak hat pattern (page 16). Hand sew a piece of heart trim across the front of the hat.

BASKET
6. Hot glue irrepressibly happy trim around the edge of a basket and then fill it with small rolls of newspaper, toys, and bones. Be sure to hot glue everything in place!

Candy Striper Tip
Volunteer with your pup! Check with your local assisted living facilities, hospitals, and rehabilitation centers to see if they could benefit from the love and affection of a pooch.

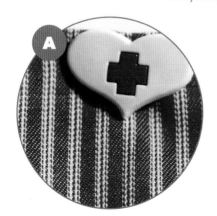

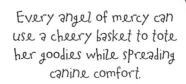

Every angel of mercy can use a cheery basket to tote her goodies while spreading canine comfort.

Sporty Guy

Materials

Yellow and green dog T-shirt
Orange pom-pom trim
Team button
Large number iron-on patches
Football patch

SUPPLIES & TOOLS
Basic Sewing Tool Kit
(page 9)

SIZE PICTURED: SMALL

Instructions

1. Pre-wash the T-shirt.

2. Using a ballpoint needle, sew pom-pom trim around the neckline and stitch a fun button in the center of the neck (photo A).

3. Add a player number and sporty details by using large iron-ons and sports-themed patches.

Sporty Guy Tip

Skip the iron-on patches. Player numbers can easily be painted on the T-shirt with fabric paint and a stencil.

Materials

DRESS
Dress pattern (page 116)
Orange curly faux fur
Yellow satin lining
Vintage green taffeta
Kelly-green sequin trim
Yellow star buttons

SUPPLIES & TOOLS
Freezer paper
Craft knife
Paintbrush
5-inch (12.7 cm) piece of cardboard
Basic Sewing Tool Kit (page 9)

ACCESSORIES
Megaphone patch: Felt, glitter paint, and rhinestones
Pom-poms: Yellow and orange yarn, cardboard, and wide sequin trim

SIZE PICTURED: WIDE MEDIUM

Instructions

DRESS

1. Cut out the top portion of the dress as described in the doggie dress pattern (page 11).

2. Instead of gathering the skirt piece, create a large box pleat in the center and two knife pleats on the side (photo A).

3. Stay stitch the pleats and then sew the top and skirt together.

4. Hot glue sequin trim around the waist, and hand stitch two yellow star buttons above the pleats.

5. Cut a megaphone shape from a piece of felt.

6. To paint words on the felt, trace letters onto the paper side of the freezer paper. Use a craft knife to cut out the letters, iron the paper to the felt, and paint.

7. Add glitter paint to highlight the letters. Add layers of felt, glitter paint, and rhinestones to the megaphone. Hot glue the patch to the dress.

Let your dog shake it up for the home team with pup-sized pom-poms. Wrap yellow and orange yarn around a 5-inch (12.7 cm) piece of cardboard until you have many layers, then tightly tie off one end of the wrapped yarn and cut through all the layers on the other end.

Cheerleader Tip

Kids love pom-poms just as much as canines. The same technique for the puppy pom-poms can be used to create kid-sized pom-poms. Just wrap the yarn around a 12-inch (30.5 cm) piece of cardboard.

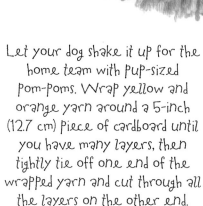

A

Materials

CAPE
Cape pattern (page 119)
Yellow vinyl
Black flame print cotton (lining)
Wide black webbing, 2 inches (5 cm) wide
Fluorescent orange webbing, 1 inch (2.5 cm) wide
Small plastic fire department toys
Toy badge

BOOTS
Shoe pattern (page 124)
Black felt
Yellow felt
Black paint
Paintbrush
Letter stencils

HAT
Small toy fireman's hat
2 yards (1.8 m) ribbon

SUPPLIES & TOOLS
Basic Sewing Tool Kit (page 9)
Hand drill

SIZE PICTURED: LARGE

Instructions

CAPE

1. Once you've cut out your pattern and fabric, sew a strip of 2-inch-wide (5 cm) black webbing across the center of the cape.

2. Sew a strip of 1-inch-wide (2.5 cm) fluorescent orange webbing on top of the black webbing. Sew one strip of orange webbing across the cape near the neck and one strip toward the bottom of the cape. Continue sewing the cape as described in the cape pattern (page 14).

3. Hot glue the fire department toys to the center strip of webbing (photo A). Hot glue a toy badge to the webbing closest to the neck.

HAT

4. Using a hand drill, drill two holes on each side of the helmet near the base.

5. Cut the ribbon into two 1-yard (.9 m) pieces. Thread the ribbon through the holes, and tie a knot for security.

BOOTS

6. Follow the instructions in the shoe pattern (page 22). Using a stencil, paint the letters "FD" down the center of the boots.

Fire Patrol Tip

Are toy hats too big for your pooch? You can easily create a fire department hat from the peak hat pattern. Just make the hat using red fabric and stencil "FD" on the front.

> Dedicated? Yes.
> In style? Always.

Dalmatian

Materials

DRESS

Dress pattern (page 116)
Black and white faux fur
Red and black paw print fabric
Red piping
Wide red sequin trim
Red mirror iron-on hearts

SUPPLIES & TOOLS

Basic Sewing Tool Kit (page 9)

Instructions

DRESS

1. Sew the dress as described in the doggie dress pattern (page 11).

2. Add red piping around the neck.

3. Attach wide red sequin trim at the waistline using hot glue or by sewing (photo A).

4. On the front near the neck, attach two iron-on hearts to the dress (photo B).

Dalmatian Tip

Make your own piping. Wrap a strip of bias fabric around a piece of thin cotton cording. Using a zipper foot, sew as close to the cording as possible, going through both layers of fabric.

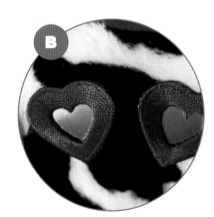

Santa Baby

There really <u>is</u> a Santa Claus, right?

Materials

CAPE

Cape pattern (page 119)
Red sequin fabric
Wide black velvet ribbon
Rhinestone buckle
White marabou trim
2 large black buttons

HAT

Cone hat pattern (page 122)
Red sequin fabric
Red taffeta (lining)
White marabou trim

SUPPLIES & TOOLS

Basic Sewing Tool Kit
  (page 9)

SIZE PICTURED: SMALL

Instructions

CAPE

1. Omitting the collar, sew the cape pattern as described in the instructions (page 14).

2. Thread the black velvet ribbon through the rhinestone buckle. Hot glue the buckle to the center and the ribbon ends to the sides of the costume.

3. Hot glue the marabou trim around the entire costume, and sew two glitzy buttons in the center above the belt (photo A).

HAT

4. Sew the hat as described in the cone hat pattern (page 17), omitting the brim.

5. Hot glue marabou trim around the base and at the very top of the hat.

Santa Baby Tip

Create a traditional Mr. Santa Claus costume by using red velvet, white faux fur trim, and a patent leather belt.

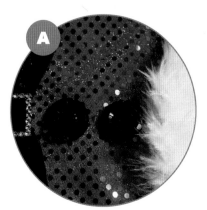

Femme Fatale

Is your pooch a princess or does she just act like one? Either way, the costumes in this chapter will surely turn your pup into a heartbreaker. Off for a trip to the mall or out practicing her moves, nothing's too good for your sassy little lady.

Canine Couture

Creating ultra-fem accents for your darling is a simple matter of pink, purple, and a whole lot of sparkle. Posh is a must-have in any doggie diva's wardrobe, providing the ultimate in everyday glamour. Lazy Daisy, Glitz, and Victorian rely on subtler feminine accents like flowers, crystals, and bows.

Glitz

Posh

Lazy Daisy

Victorian

Tiny Dancer

Materials

DRESS

Dress pattern (page 116)
2 shades of blue raw silk (top)
Cream flannel (lining)
2 shades of blue tulle (skirt)
Sheer metallic star organza
   (skirt)
Velvet trim
Blue silk flower
Vintage-style shank button

LEGWARMERS

Light lilac knit fabric

SUPPLIES & TOOLS

Basic Sewing Tool Kit (page 9)

SIZE PICTURED: EXTRA SMALL

Instructions

DRESS

1. Sew the top portion of the dress as described in the doggie dress pattern (page 11) using the blue silk.

2. Create the skirt by layering the tulle and organza fabric. Gather your layers across the top edge, and sew it along the front bottom edge of the silk top.

3. Cut slices into the bottom edge of the skirt. Evenly space the cuts across the skirt for maximum fluffiness.

4. Hot glue velvet trim along the waist, covering the stitch line (photo A).

5. Pull apart the petals on a silk flower, and layer the petals together near the neckline. Thread a shank button through the hole on the petals and hand stitch it to the dress (photo B).

LEGWARMERS

6. First, measure the height of the leg, adding length to the measurement if you want the scrunchy look. Measure around the thickest part of the leg, and add an inch.

7. Cut a rectangle of the light lilac fabric—knit fabrics work best—to the determined measurements. Fold the rectangle in half, and sew the seam closed.

Tiny Dancer Tip

Create a princess costume by creating the dancer costume and adding jewels around the neck. Sew a matching peak hat and add lots of glitter and rhinestones to create a crown.

French Maid

Do you want a chocolate on your pillow or may I lick your feet?

Materials

DRESS
Dress pattern (page 116)
Black shiny fabric
Sheer white double-edge ruffled trim
4-inch-wide (10.2 cm) white ruffle lace trim (apron)
Black sequin trim
White dog bone button

HAT
Peak hat pattern (page 121)
Black shiny fabric
Small white lace trim
Black sequin trim

ACCESSORIES
Feather duster: feather pick, small doily, and black ribbon

SUPPLIES & TOOLS
Basic Sewing Tool Kit (page 9)

SIZE PICTURED: WIDE MEDIUM

Instructions

DRESS

1. Sew the top and skirt portions of the dress as described in the doggie dress pattern (page 11).

2. Create the apron by cutting two equal length pieces of wide lace trim. With the lace facing opposite directions, sew the pieces to the center of the dress.

3. Sew the double-ruffle trim on both sides of the apron to create faux apron straps.

4. Attach the double-ruffle trim around the edge of the neckline, waist, and hem. Hot glue the black sequin trim down the center of the ruffle.

5. Sew a bone-shaped button on the top center of the dress (photo A).

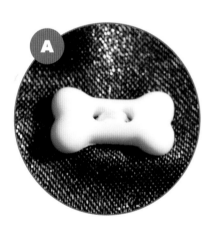

HAT

6. Follow the instructions as described in the peak hat pattern (page 16).

7. Add small lace trim and a band of sequins to the top edge with hot glue or by hand sewing.

FEATHER DUSTER

8. Fold the end of a feather pick in half to create a handle. Thread the handle through the center of a doily, and hot glue the pick in place. Add a bow made with black ribbon.

French Maid Tip

Make your own double ruffle trim! Sew a gather stitch down the center of sheer ribbon. Pull the threads to create a gather and you have double-ruffle trim.

Red Hat Ladies

Sassy

Materials

DRESS
Dress pattern (page 116)
Sheer ribbon-embellished fabric
Faux suede lining
Red feather boa
Purple tulle
Gold sequins and trim
Red rhinestone buttons

HAT
Wide-brim doll hat
Red paint
Gold sequin trim
Red feather boa
Red felt

SUPPLIES & TOOLS
Basic Sewing Tool Kit (page 9)
Paintbrush

SIZE PICTURED: EXTRA LARGE

Instructions

DRESS
1. Making the skirt slightly shorter, sew the top and skirt portion of the dress as described in the doggie dress pattern (page 11).

2. Hot glue a feather boa around the neck so that it forms a "V" shape.

3. Create a fluffy tulle collar by gathering a long strip of 6-inch-wide (15.2 cm) tulle down the center and stitching it to the top of the dress. Hot glue sequin trim over the stitch line, and hand sew on two rhinestone buttons (photo A).

4. Sew gathered tulle around the waist, and hot glue sequin trim over the stitch line.

HAT
5. Paint the wide-brim doll-sized hat with red paint, covering both sides.

6. Hot glue the gold sequin trim around the edge of the brim, and add a feather boa around the base of the hat.

7. Cut a piece of elastic to the appropriate size for a chin strap. Hand sew the ends of the elastic to the inside edges of the hat. If the hat scratches your dog's head, cover the inside brim with a circle of felt using glue.

Sassy Tip
No need to cut tulle into strips. Buy 6-inch-wide (15.2 cm) tulle on spools. You can get many yards for just a few dollars.

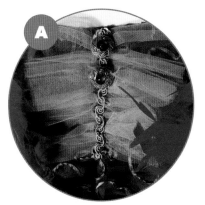

Sophisticated Lady

Materials

DRESS

Dress pattern (page 116)
Purple faux suede
Purple star ribbon
Plastic rhinestone buckle
Red ribbon
Silver beaded trim
Dark purple marabou trim

HAT

9-inch (22.9 cm) boater hat
Red paint
Purple star ribbon
Dark purple marabou trim
Large red silk rose

SUPPLIES & TOOLS

Basic Sewing Tool Kit
    (page 9)
Paintbrush

SIZE PICTURED: MEDIUM

Instructions

DRESS

1. Sew the top and skirt portion of the dress as described in the doggie dress pattern (page 11).

2. Create the belt by measuring across the top of the dress at the waist. Cut a piece of 2-inch-wide (5 cm) star ribbon to the measurement. Thread the ribbon through a rhinestone buckle, threading a smaller piece of red ribbon through the buckle for extra pop (photo A).

3. Pin and sew the edges of the ribbon into the side seam of the top of the dress. Add a drop of hot glue behind the buckle for security.

4. Hand sew the ends of a 12-inch (30.5 cm) piece of beaded trim to the neckline to create a necklace.

5. Hot glue marabou trim around the armholes and waist, and attach a strip of star ribbon to the skirt's hem.

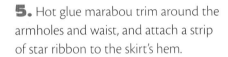

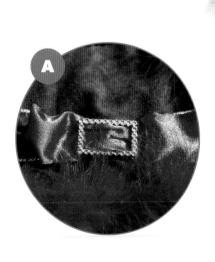

HAT

6. Begin by painting the boater hat with red paint, covering both sides.

7. Pierce a hole on both sides of the hat, and thread a long ribbon through the holes to create a chin strap. Secure the ends with a knot at the hole.

8. Hot glue a large red silk rose on the top of the hat, and add dark purple marabou trim around the base.

Sophisticated Tip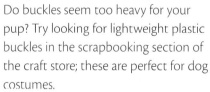

Do buckles seem too heavy for your pup? Try looking for lightweight plastic buckles in the scrapbooking section of the craft store; these are perfect for dog costumes.

Beverly Hills Valley Girl

Materials

DRESS

Dress pattern (page 116)
Tan and cream houndstooth
    fabric
Black lace
Black velvet braid trim
Velvet flocked roses
Beaded silk ribbon flower
Iron-on dog patch
Topaz and orange rhinestones
Jump rings
Heart and cupid charms
Gold crocheted chain
2 gold and pearl buttons

SHOES

Shoe pattern (page 124)
Tan and cream houndstooth
    fabric
Black felt
2 beaded silk ribbon flowers

SUPPLIES & TOOLS

Basic Sewing Tool Kit (page 9)
Rhinestone setter

SIZE PICTURED: SMALL

Instructions

DRESS

1. Sew the top and skirt portions of the dress as described in the doggie dress pattern (page 11), adding a layer of black lace to the top of the skirt prior to attaching it to the dress top.

2. Sew the velvet braid trim around the entire top portion of the dress. Glue or stitch a ribbon flower to the center of the neck (photo A).

3. Iron on the dog patch, and randomly attach rhinestones using a setter.

4. Using jump rings, attach charms to the gold crocheted chain or to the trim (photo B). Sew each end of the chain to the sides of the skirt, and add a large pearl button.

SHOES

5. Create the shoes by following the instructions in the shoe pattern (page 22).

6. Add the houndstooth fabric to the top portion of each shoe. Glue or hand sew the beaded ribbon flower to the center of both shoes.

Beverly Hills Tip

Make your own ribbon rosettes. Gather the edge of 1½ yards (1.4 m) of 2½-inch-wide (6.4 cm) wired ribbon, roll the ribbon, and hand stitch one edge of the roll together as you continue rolling. Begin with a tight roll, and loosen it as you reach the end.

Traditional

What doggy costume book would be complete without a salute to the tried and true? But make no mistake; traditional is anything but boring with these fabulous doggy outfits. From a special space cadet to one peace-loving pooch, this collection has something for everyone.

Canine Couture

Paired with traditional dog costumes or standing alone, these collars and leashes are great everyday options. In Bow Wow Bows, bone buttons and paw print ribbon join forces for a classic take on canine fashion. Use faux leather trim and a bandana bow to make the western-inspired Giddy Up or create the perfect plaid-accented Par Four for your favorite little caddy.

Bow Wow Bows

Giddy Up

Par Four

GOLF

The Cowboy

Materials

CAPE

Cape pattern (page 119)
Red bandana fabric
Lightweight denim (pants)
Tan faux suede (chaps and vest)
Faux suede fringe
8 nailhead studs
Toy cowboy belt
2 brushed-metal buttons
Toy sheriff's badge and handcuffs

HAT

Doll-sized cowboy hat
Toy sheriff's badge
Faux leather trim

ACCESSORIES

Blue bandana
   (store-bought
   or homemade)

SUPPLIES & TOOLS

Basic Sewing Tool Kit (page 9)

SIZE PICTURED: LARGE

Instructions

CAPE

1. Cut out the cape pattern from the bandana print fabric, omitting the collar.

2. Layer the denim fabric over the bottom section of the bandana print fabric to create the pants.

3. Create a chap shape by cutting a piece of faux suede that is the same size as the denim section. At the bottom center of the suede piece, cut out a large triangle to create two legs. Layer and sew the faux suede over the denim.

4. On the top section, add faux suede in the shape of a vest. Finish sewing the cape following the cape pattern instructions (page 14).

5. Sew fringe around the side edge of the chaps, attach 4 nail heads to each chap. Sew fringe and glue a toy belt across the top of the chaps. Hand sew a pair of plastic handcuffs to the waist.

6. Sew 2 buttons in the center of the vest and glue a sheriff's badge at the chest.

HAT

7. Begin with a doll-sized straw cowboy hat and poke two holes in the sides. Cut a piece of elastic to the appropriate size, thread it through the holes, and tie off the ends with a knot, adding a drop of glue for extra security.

8. Glue trim around the base of the hat and a toy sheriff's badge in the center front of the hat.

9. For added cowboy attitude, fold a bandana into a triangle and tie it around your dog's neck.

Cowboy Tip

Attaching nailheads is a snap with a pencil. Use the eraser to bend back the prongs.

The Cowgirl

DRESS
Dress pattern (page 116)
Tan faux suede
Western print cotton
Brown faux suede fringe
Silver star studs

HAT
Doll-sized straw hat
Silk daisy flowers

BOOTS
Shoe pattern (page 124)
Tan felt
Faux suede fringe
Western print cotton

SUPPLIES & TOOLS
Basic Sewing Tool Kit (page 9)
Fusible webbing
Pinking shears

SIZE PICTURED: MEDIUM

Instructions

DRESS

1. Before sewing the doggie dress, make a second copy of the top front dress pattern and create a western-style pointed yoke on it. Cut out the pattern piece.

2. Apply paper-backed fusible webbing to the back of the faux suede, pin on the paper pattern, and cut out the yoke shape. Once you've removed the paper from the yoke, fuse it to the front of the dress with an iron.

3. Sew the top and skirt portions of the dress as described in the doggie dress pattern (page 11).

4. Sew suede fringe around the waist and the skirt hem (photo A).

5. Add star studs to the points on the yoke by piercing the prongs through the fabric and then using a pencil eraser to bend the prongs back (photo B).

HAT

6. Poke two holes in the sides of a doll-sized straw hat. Cut a piece of elastic to the appropriate size, thread it through the holes in the hat, and tie off the ends with a knot. Consider adding a drop of glue for extra security.

7. Hot glue silk daisies around the brim.

8. Using pinking shears, cut a square shape from an old bandana and tie it around your dog's neck for an authentic Old West feel.

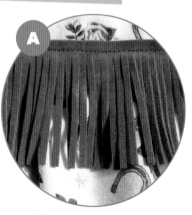

BOOTS

9. Follow the sewing instructions in the shoes pattern (page 22).

10. Embellish the boots by sewing fringe trim to the top edge. Apply fusible webbing to the back of the western print, cut out a design, and iron it to the toe portion of the boots (photo C).

Cowgirl Tip

Faux suede trim not in your budget? Make your own. Simply cut faux suede fabric into strips, and use detail scissors to cut the fringe.

Garden Fairy

Materials

DRESS

Dress pattern (page 116)
Cream cotton flannel
Yellow ribbon
6-inch-wide (15.2 cm) pale
  yellow tulle (skirt)
Light pink tulle fringe
Silk flowers and leaves
Glitter glue
Ribbon rosettes
Feather butterflies

WINGS

6-inch-wide (15.2 cm) pale
  yellow tulle
Yellow ribbon
Silk flowers

SUPPLIES & TOOLS

Basic Sewing Tool Kit
  (page 9)

SIZE PICTURED: WIDE MEDIUM

Instructions

DRESS

1. Sew the top portion of the dress as described in the doggie dress pattern (page 11). For this costume, I used a ribbon tie instead of hook-and-loop tape for the closure (photo A).

2. Create the skirt by using nine layers of tulle instead of fabric. Gather the tulle layers across the top edge, and sew it directly to the top of the dress along the front bottom edge.

3. Attach pink tulle fringe around the neckline and waist.

I love tulips!

4. Hot glue flower petals all over the top of the dress, mixing flower colors and styles (photo B). Add a drop of glitter glue in the center of each flower.

5. Hot glue three large, evenly spaced silk leaves over the top of the skirt. On top of the leaves, add two feather butterflies, layers of flower petals, and ribbon rosettes (photo C).

WINGS

6. Gather a few layers of tulle together in the center, and tie them with a ribbon to create a bow shape.

7. Hot glue the tulle bow to the center of the dress, and add flowers to the center of the bow (photo D).

Garden Fairy Tip

Create a garden angel by using white and cream flowers with gold glitter centers. Sew a base hat with white felt, add a gold pipe cleaner halo, and you've got an angel.

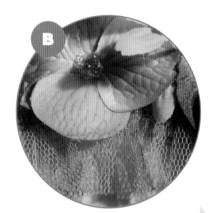

Peace. Love. Biscuits.

Materials

DRESS
Dress pattern (page 116)
Tie-dyed fabric with metallic foil butterflies
Hot pink crushed velvet (skirt)
Yellow daisy appliqué trim
Long purple fringe
Hippy patches
Silk daisies

BELT
Purple faux suede
Embroidered ribbon
Leather lacing
Beads

HEADBAND
Base hat pattern (page 121)
Hot pink crushed velvet
Silk daisies
Hippy patches

SUPPLIES & TOOLS
Basic Sewing Tool Kit (page 9)
Eyelets and setter

SIZE PICTURED: MEDIUM

Instructions

DRESS

1. Sew the top and skirt portions of the dress as described in the doggie dress pattern (page 11), adding a belt in the side seams before you assemble the dress top.

2. Create the belt pattern on a piece of scrap paper based on the following measurements.

EXTRA SMALL:
4 x 1½ inches (10.2 x 3.8 cm)

SMALL:
5 x 2 inches (12.7 x 5 cm)

MEDIUM:
6 x 2½ inches (15.2 x 6.4 cm)

WIDE MEDIUM:
7 x 3 inches (17.8 x 7.6 cm)

LARGE:
9 x 4 inches (22.9 x 10.2 cm)

EXTRA LARGE:
11 x 5 inches (27.9 x 12.7 cm)

3. Cut four pieces from the faux suede fabric. Layer two suede pieces, right sides together, and sew around the outer edge, leaving an opening on one end for turning. Clip the seams, and turn the fabric right side out. Repeat with the other two suede pieces.

4. Sew a strip of decorative ribbon down the center of the belt, and add three evenly spaced eyelets to the end that is sewn closed. Repeat for the other side of the belt.

5. Add the belt pieces to the side seam prior to sewing the top front of the dress. Thread leather lacing through the eyelets (like a shoelace), and tie decorative beads to the ends. Sew fringe over the seam connecting the top to the skirt (photo A).

6. Sew or glue yellow daisy appliqué trim around the edge of the neckline.

7. Sew, glue, or iron-on the hippy patches to the top of the dress (photo B).

8. Pull apart the petals on a silk daisy. Layer the petals with a daisy appliqué on top, and stitch the flowers to the dress, going through all layers.

Headband

9. Create the headband as described in the base hat pattern (page 18). Hot glue three silk daisies across the band. For a final, psychedelic touch, add a peace sign and daisy patches.

Hippy Dippy Tip

Create your own tie-dyed patterns using natural fiber fabric. Wet and accordion fold the fabric, wrapping rubber bands around the fold every few inches. Mix fabric dye according to the manufacturer's instructions, and place the fabric in the dye bath. Let the fabric soak, rinse it, and remove the rubber bands. Wash the fabric in cold water, and, presto, you've got a peaceful pooch.

Queen Bee

NO SEW

Materials

Black dog T-shirt
Yellow and black trim
72 x 16-inch (182.9 x 40.6 cm)
   piece of yellow netting

HAT
Base hat pattern (page 121)
Black velvet
2 fuzzy pipe cleaners
4 yellow pom-poms

SUPPLIES & TOOLS
Tailor's chalk
Basic Sewing Tool Kit (page 9)

SIZE PICTURED: MEDIUM

Instructions

1. Fold the T-shirt in half lengthwise. Using tailor's chalk, mark four parallel lines around the T-shirt.

2. Using a ballpoint needle, sew the trim around the T-shirt using a zigzag stitch on the marked lines. Gently stretch the T-shirt as you attach the trim.

3. Create wings by gathering the netting down the center. Hand stitch a piece of trim around the center, and hot glue the wings to the T-shirt.

4. Create the antennas by making the base hat (page 18) with black velvet.

5. Twist the two pipe cleaners together, and bend each end into a flat spiral shape. Hot glue pom-poms onto each side of the spiral.

6. Fold the pipe cleaners into an antenna shape, and attach a small section in the center to the hat base with hot glue and a stitch.

Queen Bee Tip
You can easily customize this outfit to make a number of flying friends if a bee doesn't suit your puppy. Try a dragonfly, a housefly, or a beetle. Whatever insect you make, use ballpoint needles; they won't tear the knit T-shirt fabric.

One giant paw print for dogkind...

Materials

CAPE

Cape pattern (page 119)
Silver tissue lamé
Clear vinyl
4 large snaps
Metallic blue ruffle trim
Red sequin trim
Red and silver holographic
    star fabric
2 blue star patches

HELMET

Small plastic food container
Wide red sequin trim
Silver sequin trim
14 medium royal-blue
    pom-poms
9 medium light blue
    pom-poms
4 small light blue pom-poms
14-inch (35.6 cm) wire star
    garland

ACCESSORIES

Small toy
Sequin scraps

SUPPLIES & TOOLS

Basic Sewing Tool Kit
    (page 9)
Hand drill

SIZE PICTURED: MEDIUM

Instructions

CAPE

1. Cut the cape pattern from clear vinyl and silver tissue lamé.

2. Baste the two pieces together by hand sewing around the outer edge.

3. Continue by sewing the cape as described in the cape pattern (page 14). For this costume, I skipped the hook-and-loop tape and used four large snaps instead.

4. Hand sew the blue ruffle trim around the edge of the collar and down the center of the cape.

5. Sew the red sequin trim around the edge of the cape and down the center of the cape on top of the blue ruffle (photo A).

6. Hot glue or sew two star patches in the corners of the cape (photo B).

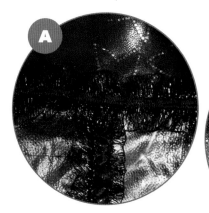

HELMET

7. Drill holes in each side of the plastic food container for elastic straps.

8. Using the elastic guide, cut a piece of elastic to the appropriate size, thread it through the holes, and tie off the ends with a knot. Add a drop of glue for extra security.

9. Hot glue the sequin trims and medium pom-poms around the base of the hat. Coil one end of the wired star garland, and hot glue the coil to the top of the hat. Then cover the coil with the remaining pom-poms, and glue the other end in the sequin trim near the base.

Earth to Scotty, do you read me? Beam up more kibble.

Astronaut Tip

Snaps give this costume a more space-age effect, but you can use hook-and-loop tape to secure the costume on your brave traveler.

You never know if those little green men are going to be your new best friend or if they need an attitude adjustment. Just in case, it wouldn't hurt to be packing a glittery laser. Make one quicker than you can say "Buck Rogers" by hot gluing sequin scraps around a toy.

Clown Around

Traditional

Materials

DRESS

Dress pattern (page 116)
Purple satin with flocked swirls
Red and orange dragon brocade
Lime-green and metallic fabric
Teal satin with flocked swirls
Sheer raspberry-pink fabric with glitter dots
Blue sequin trim
Gold bows
Yellow pom-poms
Lime-green ribbon and sequin trim
Purple felt jester trim
Marabou trim
Pink glitter pom-poms
Turquoise metallic sequin trim
Baby-blue glitter pom-poms

HAT

Cone hat pattern (page 122)
Teal satin with flocked swirls
Purple felt
Yellow pom-poms
Lime-green sequin trim
Iridescent blue sequin trim
1 hot-pink pom-pom

RUFFLES

Ruffles pattern (page 19)
Purple and teal satin with flocked swirls

SUPPLIES & TOOLS

Basic Sewing Tool Kit (page 9)

SIZE PICTURED: LARGE

Instructions

DRESS

1. Alter the top front dress pattern by adding ½ inch (1.3 cm) to the fold side. Do not cut the top front piece on the fold. Cut each piece from a different color of fabric.

2. Sew the two top front dress pieces together down the center seam with a ½-inch (1.3 cm) seam allowance. Continue assembling the dress as described in the pattern instructions (page 11).

3. Begin embellishing the dress by gluing wide blue sequin trim down the center front of the dress; add gold bows and yellow pom-poms (photo A).

4. Hot glue the purple felt jester trim around the neckline with green sequin trim on top. Add a small piece of marabou trim at the center and pink pom-poms at each point on the jester trim (photo B).

5. At the waist, hot glue the jester trim, blue sequin trim, and the baby-blue pom-poms.

6. On the skirt, sew a band of the jester trim about 4 inches (10.2 cm) from the hem. Hot glue marabou trim over the stitch line, and add yellow pom-poms. Sew the pink double ruffle trim to the hem, and hot glue the green sequin trim down the center of the ruffle trim (photo C).

HAT

7. Create the hat as described in the cone hat pattern (page 17), omitting the brim.

8. Hot glue a purple felt triangle in the center front, and add green sequin trim around the bottom edge and blue sequin trim to the tip of the hat.

9. Attach two yellow pom-poms to the center of the hat and one on the top.

RUFFLES

10. Create the ruffles as described in the ruffles pattern (page 19).

Clown Around Tip

A clown costume is a great way to use up colorful scraps of fabric and trim.

I draw the line at the red nose.

Spooky

Even if your dog couldn't scare a rabbit, he can still vamp it up in style. One part spooky and one part kooky, your devilishly cute pup will turn heads, send chills up the spine, or maybe just illicit some laughs in these classic costumes.

Canine Couture

Does your pooch like to ham it up for the holidays? Get in touch with Lucky's spookier side with bright orange pom-poms, Halloween-themed ribbons, and buttons in Pumpkin Fun and Trick or Treat. For a creepy-crawly look on the lighter side, try Lady Love Bug.

Lady Love Bug

Pumpkin Fun

Trick or Treat

Vampire

Materials

CAPE
Cape pattern (page 119)
Black stretch velvet fabric
Red stretch velvet fabric (collar)
Black bat print fabric (lining and side flaps)
White glitter felt
Silver sequin trim
Gothic necklace
Spider web charms
Bat buttons

RUFFLES
Ruffles pattern (page 19)
Red holographic star fabric

SUPPLIES & TOOLS
Basic Sewing Tool Kit (page 9)

SIZE PICTURED: LARGE

Instructions

CAPE

1. Sew the cape following the pattern instructions (page 14).

2. Cut the white felt square into a long triangle, and hot glue or sew it down the top center of the cape.

3. Decorate the edge of the felt triangle with silver sequin trim. Attach a gothic necklace so it lies in the center of the felt (photo A).

4. Sew a spider charm and a bat button onto the corners of the collar (photo B).

RUFFLES

5. Sew the ruffles as described in the ruffles pattern (page 19).

Vampire Tip

Avoid human vampires by eating tons of great food marinated in garlic, although you may need a different approach for canine counts.

Materials

CAPE
Cape pattern (page 119)
Red taffeta fabric
Red metallic fabric (lining)
Black sequin trim
Flame fabric
Gold glitter paint
Red glitter paint

HORNS
Base hat pattern (page 121)
Devil horn pattern (page 124)
Red metallic fabric
Red stretch-velvet fabric
Red glitter paint

ACCESSORIES
Store-bought pitchfork

SUPPLIES & TOOLS
Basic Sewing Tool Kit (page 9)
Fusible webbing
Stuffing
Tacky glue

SIZE PICTURED: SMALL

Instructions

CAPE

1. Cut out and sew the basic cape shape as described in the cape pattern instructions (page 14).

2. Add black sequin trim around the edge of the collar.

3. To create the cape's flames, apply fusible webbing to the back of the flame fabric. Cut out the flames, and attach them to the cape with an iron. Add highlights to the flames by outlining them with red and gold glitter paint (photo A).

HORNS

4. Sew the base as described in the base hat pattern (page 18).

5. Using the devil horn pattern, cut four devil horn pieces from red velvet. Place the pieces right sides together, sew down the two side edges, and clip the seams. Turn the fabric right side out, fill the fabric with stuffing, and hand sew the horns to the hat base. Add glitter paint around the base of the horns for extra mischievous sparkle (photo B).

A pitchfork is just the thing for poking do-gooders. Using tacky glue, apply glitter to one side of the pitchfork, and allow it to dry before adding glitter to the other side.

Devil Tip

Can't find flame fabric? Here are three ideas to try: paint your own flames with fabric paints; cut flame shapes from red, orange, and yellow felt; or look online for just the right fabric.

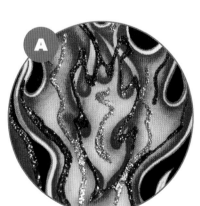

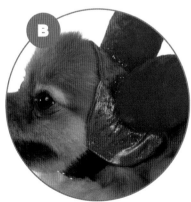

Materials

Black dog T-shirt
White fabric paint

SUPPLIES & TOOLS

Waxed paper
Medium paintbrush
Iron

SIZE PICTURED: EXTRA SMALL

Instructions

1. Prewash the T-shirt. Add a layer of waxed paper in between the top and bottom of the T-shirt to prevent the paint from bleeding through.

2. To create the spine, paint 18 stripes down the center of the T-shirt, starting with wide strokes at the top of the spine, short strokes in the middle, and wide strokes again toward the base.

3. Make the ribs by painting eight curved stripes on each side of the spine. You might want to practice painting on a piece of paper before you begin on the T-shirt.

4. Allow the shirt to dry, and heat-set the paint with an iron following the paint label instructions.

Skully Tip

No fabric paint? Create your own by blending fabric medium with acrylic craft paint.

Sea Creature

Materials

CAPE

Cape pattern (page 119)
Green low-nap faux fur
Various shades of green felt
Sea creature tail pattern
**   (page 125)**
Plastic leaves

HAT

Sea creature hat patterns
**   (page 125)**
Green low-nap faux fur
Green felt
Plastic leaves
2 plastic animal eyes

SUPPLIES & TOOLS

Stuffing
Basic Sewing Tool Kit (page 9)
Pinking shears

SIZE PICTURED: LARGE

Instructions

CAPE

1. Create the cape, minus the collar, following the pattern instructions (page 14). Alter the pattern for the top of the cape by making a second copy of the cape pattern piece and adding ½ inch (1.3 cm) to the fold edge. Do not place the pattern's fold edge on the fold when you cut the fabric; this will give you two pieces for the top of the cape. Cut out the lining using the regular pattern piece placed on the fold.

2. To create the ridge, glue or sew scraps of green felt together until you have two strips that are 5 inches (12.7 cm) wide and as long as the center of your cape piece.

3. Layer the two strips together, and topstitch a large zigzag down one side (photo A). Trim the felt close to the stitching line, and stuff each peak with a small amount of stuffing.

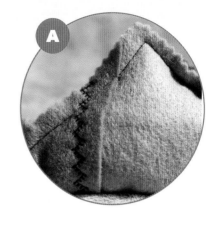

4. Working right sides together, sandwich the ridge between the two cape pieces and sew in place using a ½-inch (1.3 cm) seam allowance. Continue sewing the cape.

5. Using the sea creature tail pattern, cut two tail pieces from the faux fur. Create scales by cutting pieces of felt into large, chunky zigzags. Working on

the right side of the fabric, stitch the felt pieces across the tail, adding as many scale pieces as you wish.

6. Place the two tail piece right sides together and sew down the two side edges. Clip the corners and turn the fabric right side out.

7. Add a little stuffing to the end of the tail. Gather the fabric along the top edge, and stitch the tail to the middle bottom section of the cape. For a finishing touch, hot glue plastic leaves under the felt scales (photo B).

8. Hot glue plastic leaves around the collar area. As you did with the tail, create felt scales and hot glue them over the leaves (photo C).

HAT

9. Using the sea creature hat patterns, cut hat pattern pieces 1 and 2 from the faux fur. Cut the lining from green felt using hat pattern piece 1.

10. Create the top of the hat by sewing the two faux fur pieces together along the top curved edge with right sides facing, following the same step with felt for the lining.

11. Working right sides together, sew the top and lining together at the edges, leaving an opening for turning. Turn the fabric right side out, and hand stitch the opening closed.

12. Fold the hat on the fold line, and hand sew the animal eyes in place.

13. Create an elastic chin strap using the elastic size chart as a guide, and attach the elastic to both sides of the hat.

14. Working right sides together, sew the two bottom hat pieces together, leaving an opening for turning. Turn the fabric right side out, and hand stitch the opening closed. Gather the fabric along the top edge, and hand sew it to the inside of hat piece 1. Decorate the hat with plastic leaves (photo D).

Sea Creature Tip

Add texture to the felt by using pinking shears and decorative stitches.

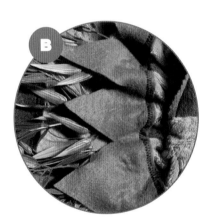

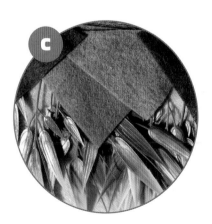

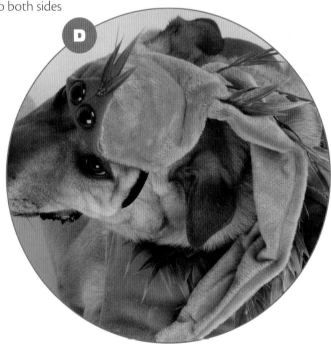

Witch's Brew

Bubble, bubble.
Am I in trouble?

Materials

DRESS
Dress pattern (page 116)
Sheer silver fabric (top)
Black glitzy fabric (lining)
Black knit fabric with gold
   threads (skirt)
Orange and black bat fabric
Lime-green rickrack trim
1-inch-wide (2.5 cm) black trim
Plastic rhinestone buckle
3 inches (7.6 cm) of black
   fringe trim
Lime-green marabou trim

HAT
Cone hat pattern (page 122)
Orange and black bat fabric
Lime green and gold fabric
Black marabou trim

BOOTS
Shoe pattern (page 124)
Black felt
Red and white striped fabric
Lime-green rickrack
Silver glitter paint
Orange felt

SUPPLIES & TOOLS
Basic Sewing Tool Kit (page 9)
Paintbrush

SIZE PICTURED: EXTRA LARGE

Instructions

DRESS

1. Sew the top and skirt portions of the dress as described in the doggie dress pattern (page 11).

2. Use scissors to cut large chunks of fabric from the hemline of the skirt for a tattered look.

3. Sew a rectangular panel of orange print fabric down the center top of the dress. If you are using fabric that frays easily, treat the edges with fray retardant prior to sewing. Sew rickrack trim in a crisscross pattern onto the rectangle to create faux lacing.

4. Add a belt by threading a piece of trim through the rhinestone buckle, and stitch it in place over the rectangular panel. Sew additional trim down the sides of the panel for a finished look (photo A).

5. Hot glue a piece of 3-inch-long (7.6 cm) black fringe around the top of the panel at the neck. Attach green marabou trim around the neckline and waist.

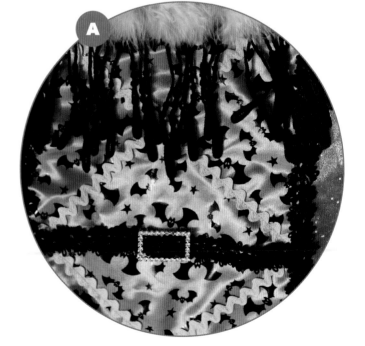

spooky

94

HAT

6. Create the hat as described in the cone hat pattern (page 17). I used lime green for the brim and orange for the cone, but you can customize the colors to suit your pooch.

7. Hot glue marabou trim around the base of the cone.

BOOTS

8. Create the boots by following the steps in the shoe pattern (page 22). Add striped fabric to the top portion, and trim the bottom edge with green rickrack.

9. Paint the toe portion of the boots with glitter paint, and glue a felt buckle shape in the center of the toe.

What's a witch without her broom? Pup-size this key witchly accoutrement by purchasing a child's toy broom. Spray paint the entire broom and then hot glue a ribbon around the length of the handle.

Witch's Brew Tip
If you cannot find knit fabric, try cutting up an old sweater or worn out blanket to create the skirt.

I'm sorry. That last batch gave me gas.

Spidey

NO SEW

Materials

Gray dog T-shirt
Dimensional glow-in-the-dark
   fabric paint
8 plastic eyes
Large black pom-pom
2 fuzzy pipe cleaners
Pin back

SUPPLIES & TOOLS

Waxed paper
Small paintbrush
Glue gun and glue sticks
Tacky glue

SIZE PICTURED: LARGE

Instructions

1. Pre-wash the T-shirt. Add a layer of waxed paper in between the top and bottom of the T-shirt so the paint doesn't bleed through.

2. Using the glow-in-the-dark paint, paint a six-pointed web shape in the center of the T-shirt. Add several layers to the web, and connect all the points together with lines that meet in the center. To make sure you get it perfect, you might want to practice on paper first.

3. Create a spider by attaching plastic eyes to a large black pom-pom with tacky glue.

4. Cut the pipe cleaners in half so you have four pieces. Center the pipe cleaners on the bottom of the pom-pom, and hot glue them in place to make legs.

5. Add a pin back to your spider with a drop of hot glue. Bend the legs and pin the spider onto the costume.

Spidey Tip

Make it washable. Adding a pin back to the spider, or any other creature of your choosing, means it can be removed for washing.

It's detachable!

Bad to the Bone

If your dog is a rebel rouser or just looks the part,
these costumes are made to order. Dressed in
these bad dude duds, no one will suspect
that his heart is really as soft as a marshmallow Peep.
Whether doing time or walking the plank, your
tough guy will be the talk of the town.

Canine Couture

These collars are perfect for the dog with a chip on his shoulder. For the ultimate statement in sassiness, fashion Punky out of leopard print ribbon, grommets, and a skull-and-crossbones button. If all your hound needs is a hint of attitude, use faux leather, an old name tag, or metal scrapbook letters to make Pinkie, Garage Dog, or Metal Max.

Garage Dog

Punky

Pinkie

Metal Max

GOth Chick

Have you seen my black eyeliner?

Materials

DRESS
Dress pattern (page 116)
Hot pink skull print fabric
Black knit fabric with metallic gold thread (skirt)
Hot pink lace
Snap tape
Plaid bow
Black felt skull
Rhinestones
Bat charm
Ball-and-chain necklace
Pink leopard print felt

SUPPLIES & TOOLS
Basic Sewing Tool Kit (page 9)
Jewelry pliers

SIZE PICTURED: EXTRA SMALL

Instructions

DRESS

1. Sew the dress as described in the doggie dress pattern (page 11).

2. Using black thread, zigzag stitch the hot pink lace around the neck and waist. Sew snap tape around the waist just above the lace.

3. Hand stitch a plaid bow made from ribbon on one side of the skirt (photo A).

4. Cut a skull shape from felt, and hand stitch it onto the top of the dress. Add features with large rhinestones, using hearts for the eyes, a star for a nose, and an upside-down moon for the mouth (photo B).

5. Add a bat charm to the ball-and-chain necklace, and attach it to the dress by hand stitching the chain at each side of the waist, securing in a few spots if needed.

6. Add a patch to the skirt by zigzag stitching around a piece of leopard print felt (photo C).

Goth Chick Tip

Using felt is a great way to save money and time, especially if you need to make patches. Felt squares are inexpensive, and the fabric won't fray.

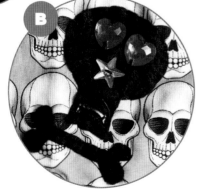

Rocker Dude

Wait for me, cherie!

Materials

CAPE
Cape pattern (page 119)
Denim
Red and gray striped fabric (shirt and flaps)
Black satin (lining)
Skull and "Fleabag" iron-on patches
Spade button
Ball-and-chain necklace
Black snap tape
Black webbing
Lime-green leopard print felt
Mahjong tile

HAT
Doll-sized newsboy hat

SUPPLIES & TOOLS
Basic Sewing Tool Kit (page 9)
Skull foam stamp
White fabric paint

SIZE PICTURED: SMALL

Instructions

CAPE

1. Omitting the collar, cut out the cape pattern from the denim. Layer the striped fabric over the top half of the denim to create the shirt, and continue sewing the costume according to the pattern instructions (page 14).

2. Attach an iron-on skull patch in the center of the shirt. Thread a spade button onto the ball-and-chain necklace, and hand sew it to the neck area.

3. Glue snap tape down the sides of the skull patch, and paint two faint skulls with a foam stamp and white fabric paint (photo A).

4. At the waist, create a belt by hot gluing webbing across the cape, and add a layer of felt on top of the webbing. Hot glue the game tile to the center for a belt buckle.

5. On the denim pants, attach a studded iron-on patch and paint a skull (photo B).

HAT

6. Cut a piece of elastic to create a chin strap. Sew each end of the elastic to the side edges of the hat.

Rocker Dude Tip

Skip buying the fabric. Go punk rock, and cut up your old jeans and band T-shirts to create this costume.

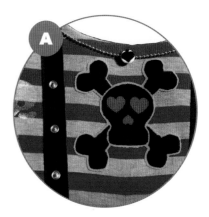

Materials

CAPE

Cape pattern (page 119)
Dollar bill print fabric
Black glitter fabric (pants and collar flaps)
Green glitter fabric (lining)
Green and gray faux fur (collar)
Gold rhinestone trim
Black glitter webbing
Gold sequin trim
Gold glitter
Gold paint
Dog bone patch
Toy wallet, money, and coins
Large gold chain
Wooden dog cutout
2 green rhinestones
Gold roping
Small gold chain
Dog bone

SUPPLIES & TOOLS

Basic Sewing Tool Kit (page 9)
Small paintbrush

SIZE PICTURED: LARGE

Instructions

CAPE

1. Cut out the cape pattern from the money print fabric and begin assembling the cape following the pattern instructions (page 14). You'll only need to cut one collar pattern piece of faux fur fabric to create the collar.

2. Working on the top of the cape, layer the black glitter fabric over the collar flap section and over the bottom half to create the pants.

3. At the top of the pants, hot glue a strip of webbing and gold rhinestone trim across the cape. Hot glue sequin trim around the outer edge of the pants.

4. To spice up the pants, iron on a dog bone patch, hot glue a toy wallet, and create a pocket with a scrap of black fabric and play money (photos A and B).

Bad to the Bone

5. Hand sew a large chain to the cape. Make a dog necklace by painting a wooden dog cutout with gold paint, adding glitter and rhinestone eyes. Sew the cutout to a piece of gold roping, and use hot glue to attach it to the cape (photo C).

6. Sew two rows of gold chain to the cape. Hot glue a gold-painted dog bone and a toy coin at the center of the chains.

Rapper Tip
Use a craft knife to cut faux fur. Working on the knit side of the fur, carefully cut through the backing without cutting the fur itself.

For added bling, place a store-bought dollar sign necklace around your dog's neck so that it hangs in the front.

C

Pirate

Bad to the Bone

107

Materials

CAPE

Cape pattern (page 119)
Cream flannel
Cream and tan frilly print
    fabric (shirt)
Burgundy faux suede (pants)
Rust skull print cotton (lining
    and side flaps)
Lace ruffled trim
Brown velvet ribbon
Pirate-themed buttons
Fishing net
Gold coin trim
Toy skull and crossbones

HAT

Peak hat pattern (page 121)
Black satin fabric
Gold and burgundy trim
White fabric paint

ACCESSORIES

Leather-wrapped toy sword
Silver hoop
Red and gold star scarf

SUPPLIES & TOOLS

Basic Sewing Tool Kit (page 9)
Foam skull stamp

SIZE PICTURED: MEDIUM

Instructions

CAPE

1. Omitting the collar, cut out the cape pattern from the cream flannel. Layer the cream and tan fabric over the top half of the flannel to create the shirt, and continue assembling the cape following the cape pattern instructions (page 14).

2. Pin 2 strips of lace trim down the center of the shirt to create the ruffles.

3. Hot glue a strip of velvet ribbon down the center of the lace. Add a row of small buttons on top of the ribbon and attach a large pirate button at the neckline (photo A).

PANTS

4. Create the pants by cutting a piece of faux suede fabric wider than the cape. Gather the piece across the top and attach it along the base of the shirt layer.

5. Sew the sides of the pants to the sides of the cape. Cut out large chunks from the bottom edge of the pants to create an aged look. In the center, slice a deep "V" shape in the fabric, and sew the edges down to form two legs (photo B).

6. Hot glue a strip of fishing net across the waist, and trim the hem of the net on an angle.

7. Glue a strip of coin trim across the net, and add additional embellishments like a pirate sword, silver hoop, skulls, and buttons by hand sewing or using hot glue (photo C).

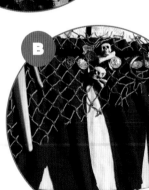

HAT

8. Follow the instructions for the peak hat pattern (page 16), and then hand sew or glue decorative trim around the peak of the hat.

9. Add a painted skull in the center of the hat by using a skull foam stamp (or stencil) and white paint.

10. Cut a rectangle of silky fabric and fold it over to create a lopsided triangle. Tie the scarf around your pup's neck for a dashing addition.

Pirate Tip

Can't find coin trim? Make your own by drilling holes in foreign coins and sewing them to a strip of ribbon.

Jail Bird

I'm innocent, I tell ya. It was Misty, the cat, who done it!

0KC82270

Materials

White dog T-shirt
Black fabric paint
Black sequin trim (wide &
    stretchy)
Craft bird
Scrap of a black feather boa

SUPPLIES & TOOLS

Basic Sewing Tool Kit (page 9)
Stencils
Foam paintbrush
Disappearing fabric pen

SIZE PICTURED: SMALL

Instructions

1. Pre-wash the T-shirt. Using a stencil and fabric paint, stencil letters onto the bottom center of the T-shirt. Heat set the paint according to the paint label instructions (photo A).

2. Fold the T-shirt in half lengthwise. Using the disappearing fabric pen and working above the stencil, mark 2 parallel lines that run around the T-shirt.

3. Using a ballpoint needle, sew the sequin trim around the T-shirt using a zigzag stitch on the marked lines. Gently stretch the T-shirt as you attach the trim.

4. Hot glue the feather boa and the craft bird to the top neck.

Jail Bird Tip

If you'd like to create a more traditional jail bird uniform with stripes, use low-tack tape to mark stripes on the shirt, and paint between the lines with fabric paint. Allow the paint to dry, remove the tape, and you will have perfect stripes.

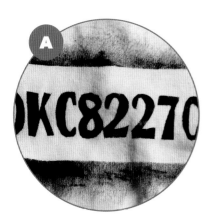

Backstage

Kudos to the dogs who took time out of their busy schedules to make this book come alive, and to their people for transporting them. A special thanks to Adelaine Lockwood, proprietor of Blaze-N-Skyy Pet Boutique, for her invaluable assistance in obtaining our talented cast of dog models. Heartfelt gratitude goes out to Halley Lawrence for her editorial wit and meticulous attention to detail.

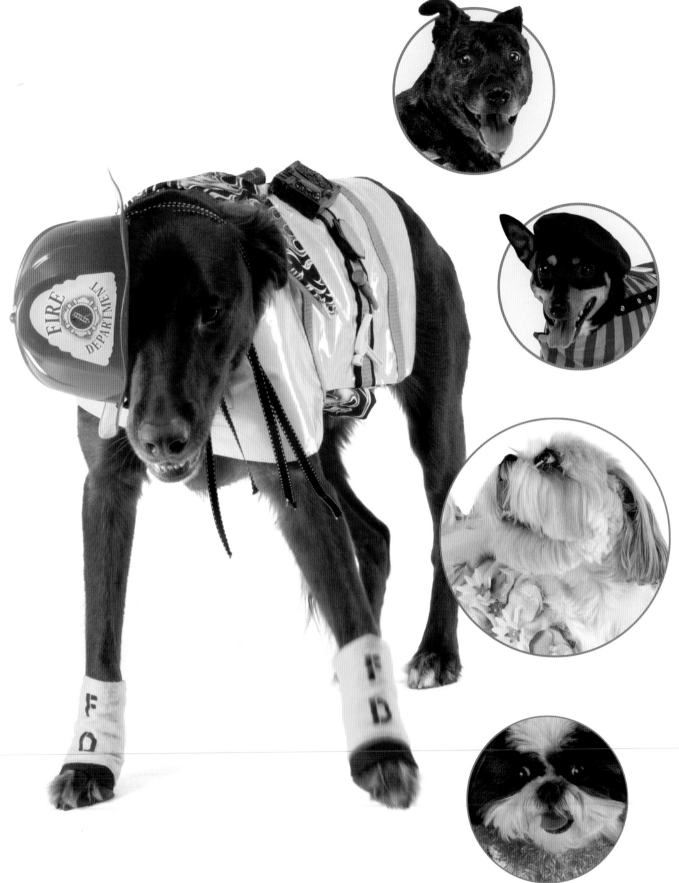

Enlarge/Reduce as needed

Dress Bodice Pieces

Extra Small: 95%

Small: 110%

Medium: 120%

Wide Medium: 135%

Large: 155%

Extra Large: 200%

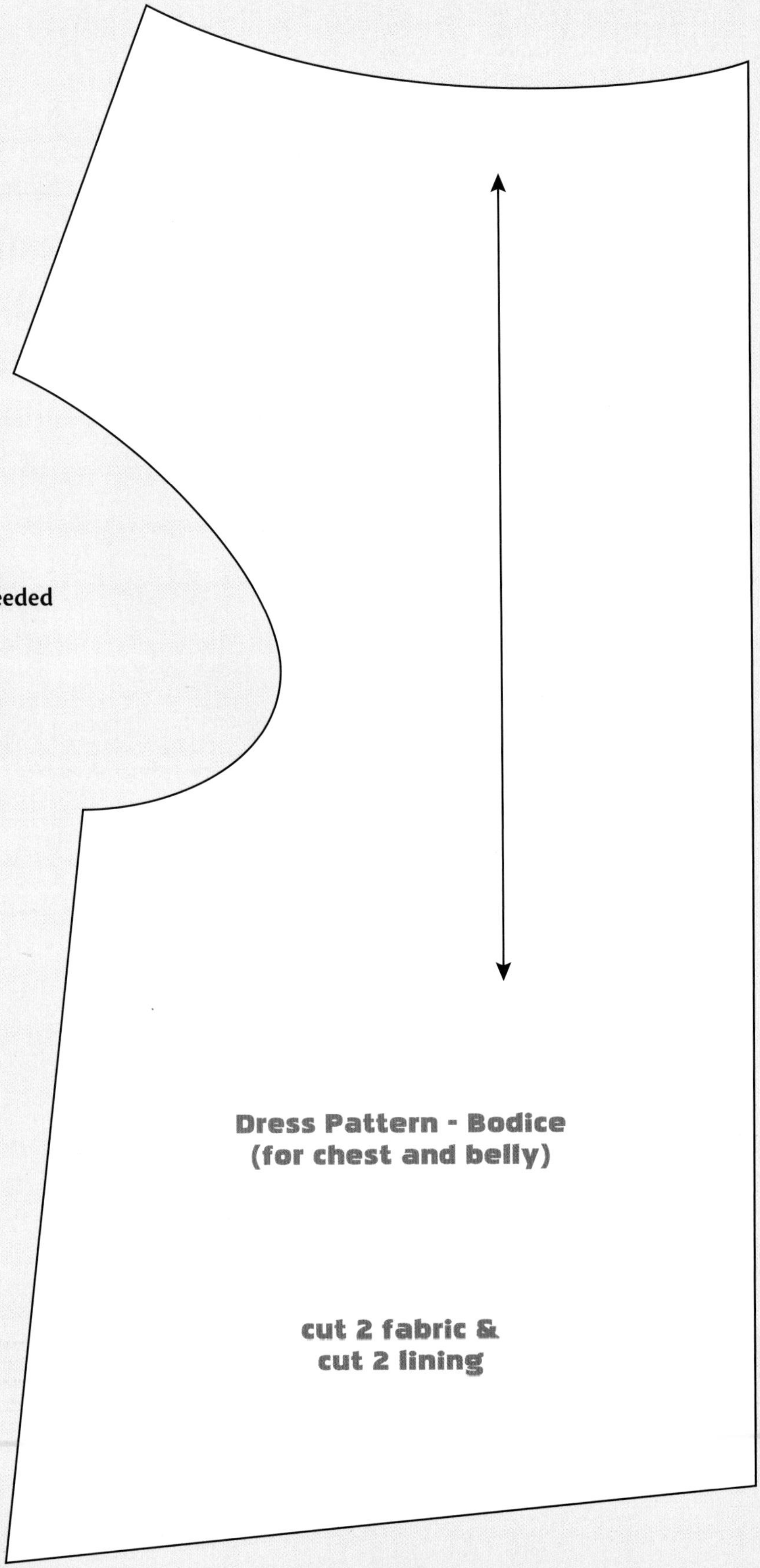

**Dress Pattern - Bodice
(for chest and belly)**

**cut 2 fabric &
cut 2 lining**

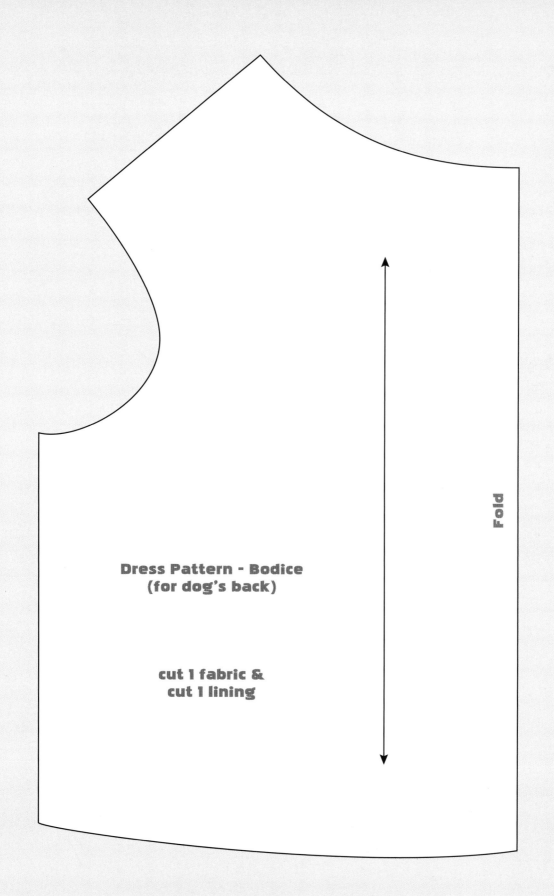

**Dress Pattern - Bodice
(for dog's back)**

**cut 1 fabric &
cut 1 lining**

Fold

Dress Pattern - Skirt

cut 1 fabric

Dress Skirt

Extra Small: 220%

Small: 270%

Medium: 300%

Wide Medium: 350%

Large: 400%

Extra Large: 500%

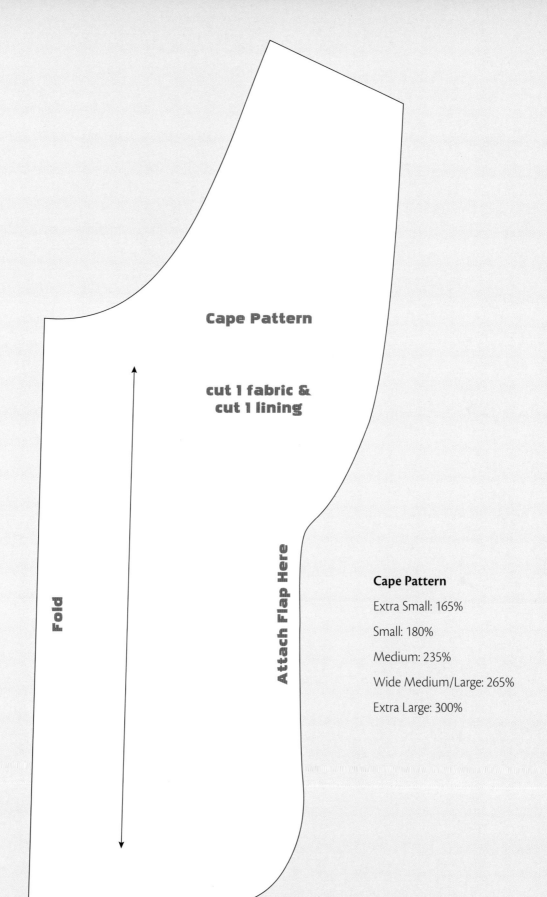

Cape Pattern

**cut 1 fabric &
cut 1 lining**

Fold

Attach Flap Here

Cape Pattern

Extra Small: 165%

Small: 180%

Medium: 235%

Wide Medium/Large: 265%

Extra Large: 300%

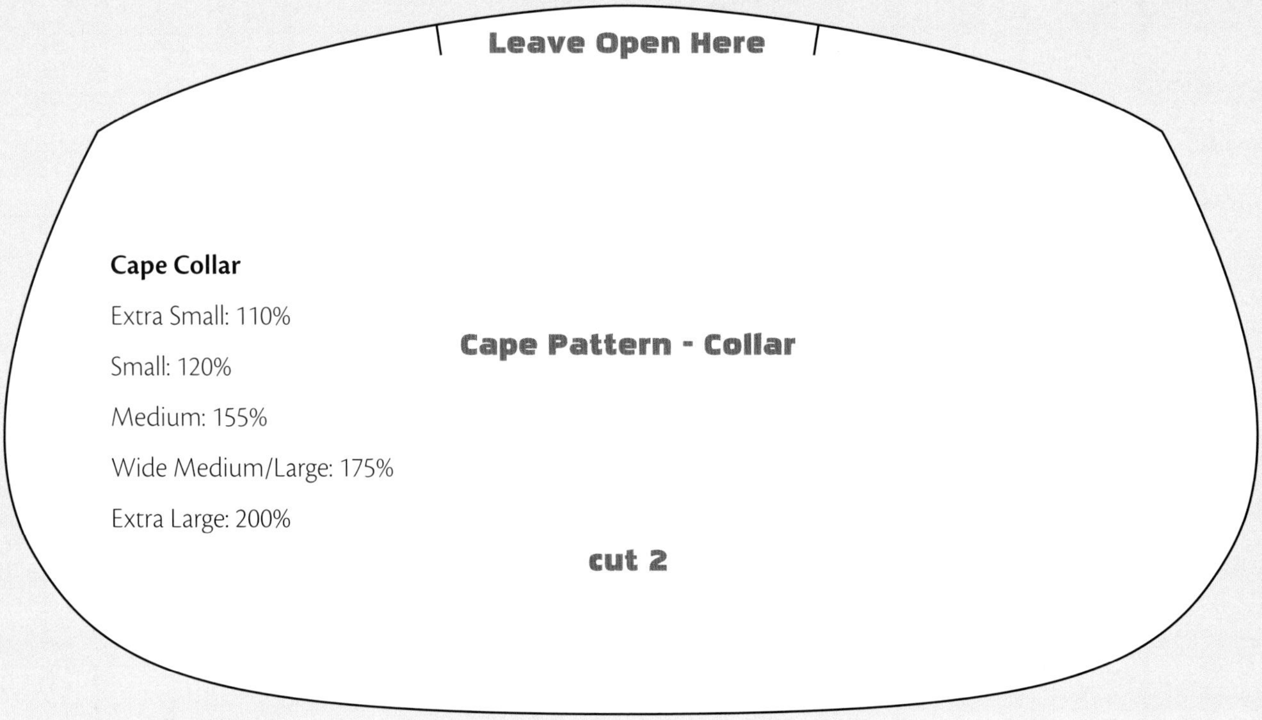

Leave Open Here

Cape Collar

Extra Small: 110%

Small: 120%

Medium: 155%

Wide Medium/Large: 175%

Extra Large: 200%

Cape Pattern - Collar

cut 2

Cape Pattern - Side Flaps

**cut 4 fabric OR
cut 2 fabric & cut 2 lining**

Cape Side Flaps

Extra Small: 100%

Small: 140%

Medium: 160%

Wide Medium/Large: 200%

Extra Large: 220%

Peak Hat

Extra Small: 90%

Small: 100%

Medium: 110%

Wide Medium: 115%

Large: 115%

Extra Large: 115%

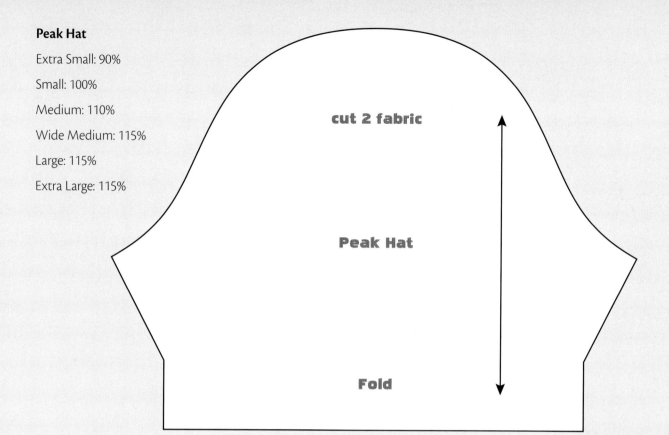

cut 2 fabric

Peak Hat

Fold

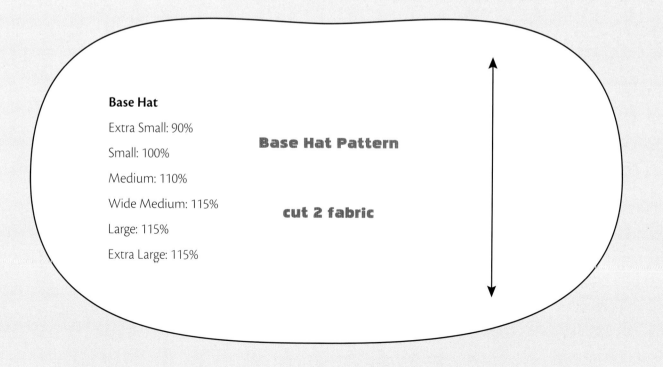

Base Hat

Extra Small: 90%

Small: 100%

Medium: 110%

Wide Medium: 115%

Large: 115%

Extra Large: 115%

Base Hat Pattern

cut 2 fabric

Cone Hat

Extra Small: 125%

Small: 125%

Medium: 135%

Wide Medium: 145%

Large: 145%

Extra Large: 145%

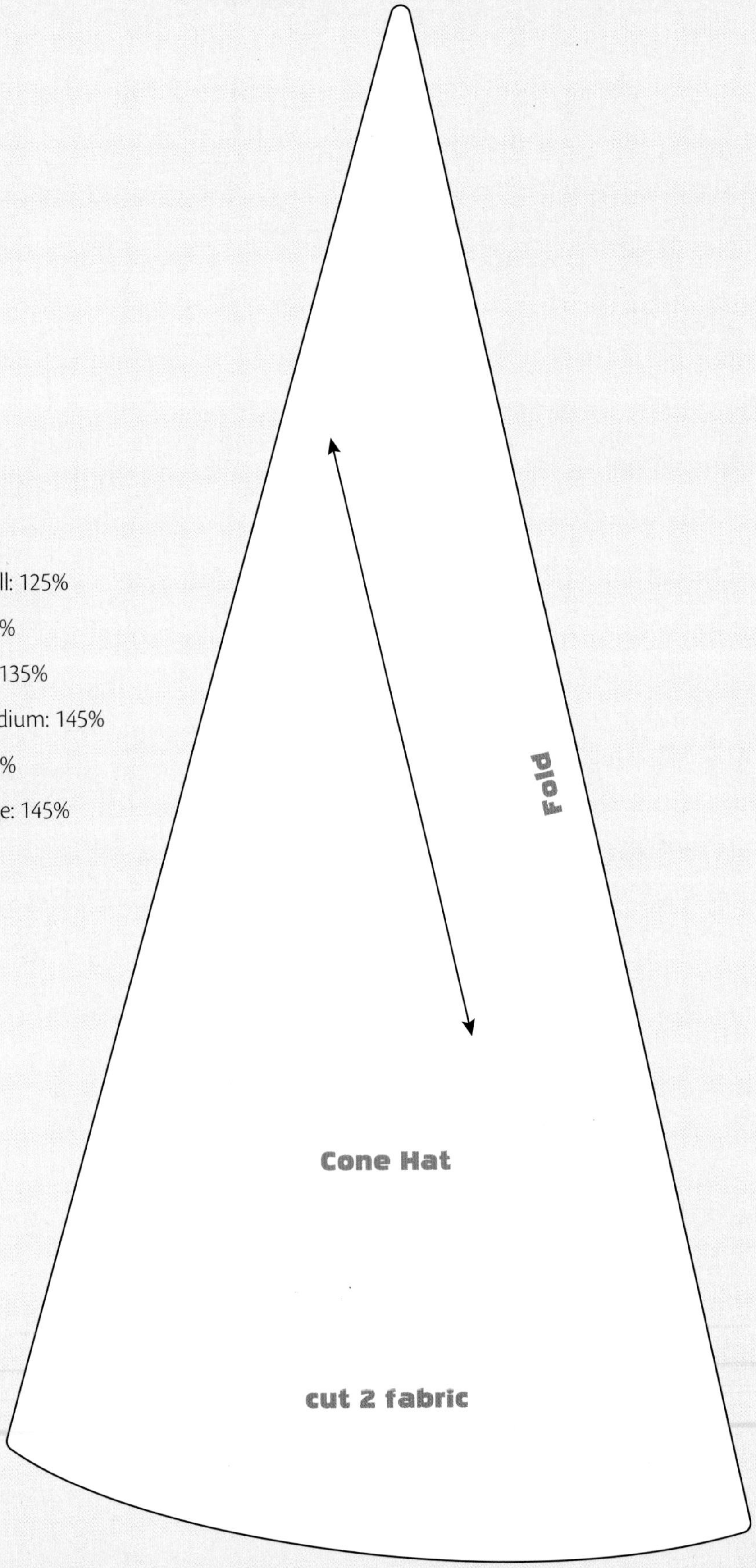

Fold

Cone Hat

cut 2 fabric

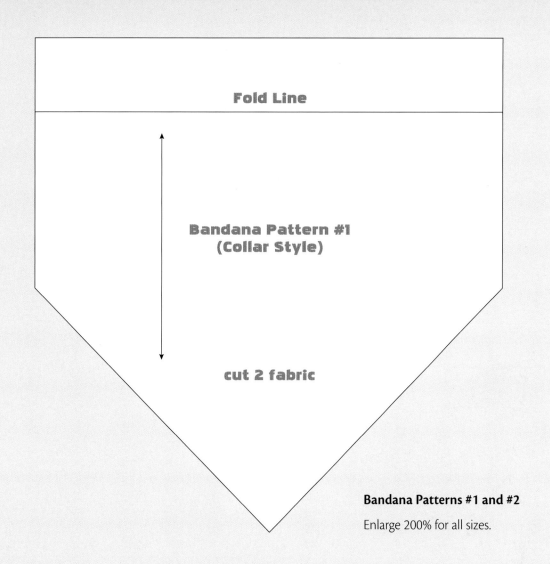

Fold Line

**Bandana Pattern #1
(Collar Style)**

cut 2 fabric

Bandana Patterns #1 and #2

Enlarge 200% for all sizes.

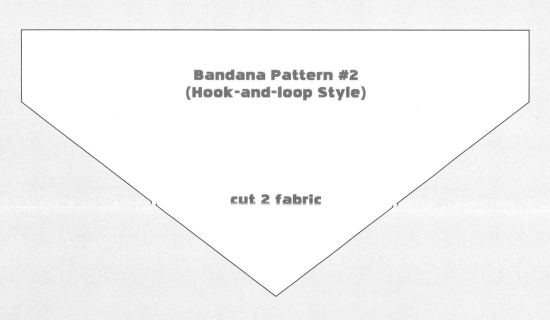

**Bandana Pattern #2
(Hook-and-loop Style)**

cut 2 fabric

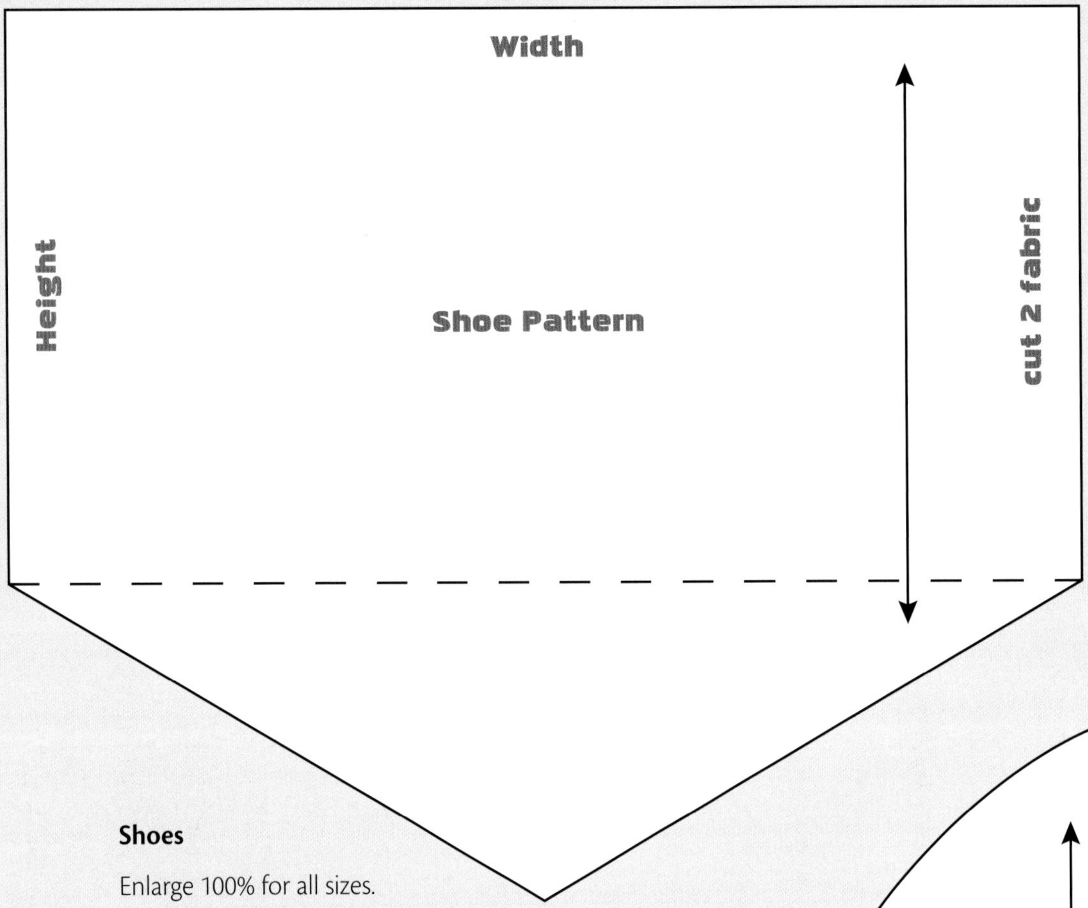

Width

Height

cut 2 fabric

Shoe Pattern

Shoes

Enlarge 100% for all sizes.

Devil Horns

cut 4 fabric

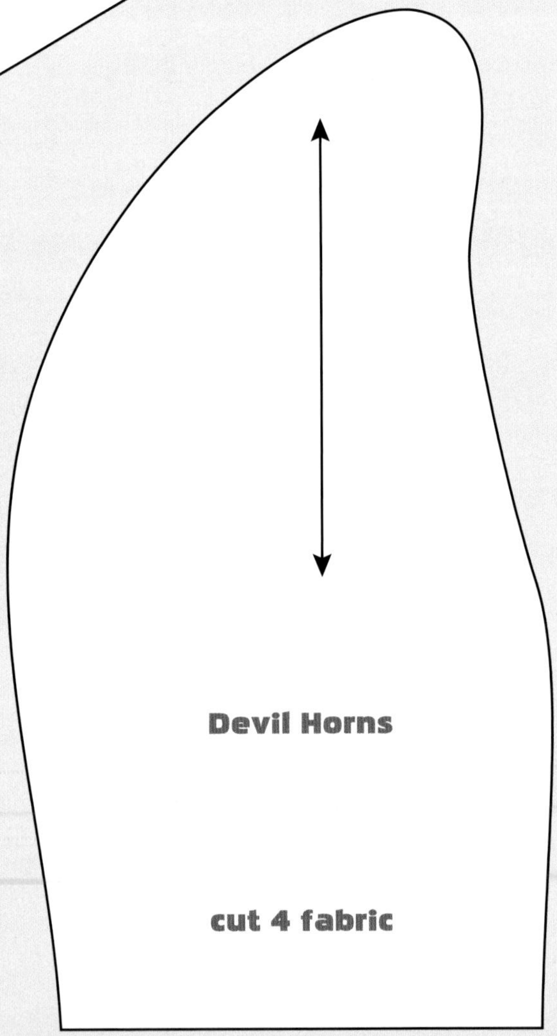

Devil Horns

Enlarge 100% for all sizes.

Sea Creature Hat Piece 2

cut 2 fabric

Sea Creature Tail

cut 2 fabric

Fold up

eyes

Sea Creature Hat Piece 1

cut 2 fabric & cut 2 lining

Sea Creature Tail and Hat Pieces

Enlarge 220% for all sizes.

Templates

Acknowledgments

A special thanks to Max Filian (my four-legged muse) for inspiring so many fun costumes and for always letting me play dress up with him. To my husband Eddie, I love you and I promise I won't dress Max as a princess anymore.
A huge thanks to all my family and friends, everyone at Lark Books, Erin Lippard, and my partners Steve Piacenza and Greg Byers. Many thanks to Gina Zycher for her awesome skull embroidery, and to Zach Driscoll for the beautiful photographs and laughs.

About the Author

Emmy-nominated Cathie Filian began sewing when she was eight, and her love of stitching followed her all the way to Ohio State University where she studied Textile Science and Fashion Design. Having worked for a time in the film business creating costumes, Cathie now serves as the creator and cohost of the popular lifestyle show *Creative Juice* on DIY Network and HGTV. The show takes a fresh look at old craft ideas with affordable and accessible projects that can inspire both the novice and advanced crafter.

Cathie's first book, *Creative Juice: 45 Re-Crafting Projects* (Lark Books, 2007), provides even more fun and funky recycled craft ideas that can be made for pennies. She also writes a monthly syndicated newspaper column for Scripps Howard News Service and contributes to national shelter publications such as *Life Magazine, Real Simple, Redbook, Quick and Simple,* and many others. Cathie lives in Los Angeles with her husband Eddie and their dog Max.

Index

"Somehow, some way, we have to guide these people back to reality!"